CONVERSATIONS WITH MY SWEETHEART ON THE OTHER SIDE

The Autobiography of Klea

A Detailed Description of Life on The Other Side

FELECIA (KLEA) and LEN (URA) LA SCOLEA

DEDICATION

This book is dedicated to Mother (Azna) and Father God.
Our Co-Creators; who we all owe our very existence too. Who
unconditionally loves all of us as their children and who has given
us the gift, the blessing of the capacity to love one another.

Acknowledgments

A special recognition to two beautiful souls, Rosemary Kristoff and David Diomede. These two books of the spiritual journey of Klea and Ura would never have been possible without the vital expertise of Rosemary and David. It is an honor to know them.

We never know how high we are

Till we are asked to rise

And then if we are true to plan

Our statures touch the skies —

EMILY DICKINSON

Our Great Frustration

It is wished that there be a transfer of our consciousness to you composing of our understandings, what has been learned and experiences the last two years with this spiritual journey. This we cannot do. It is our great frustration. To have the knowledge and understanding one can only experience for themselves. We give to you the truth within our heart of hearts and souls. The soul is the truest part of us.

KLEA AND URA

OUR ETERNAL SPIRIT NAMES

...OUR REAL NAMES

Contents

Prologue

In all our existence, in this life what can be more important than the realization of:

- ❦ Who and what we really are?
- ❦ Where did we come from?
- ❦ Why are we here on This Side?
- ❦ What is our purpose in this life?
- ❦ Where do we return to?

Knowing these truths within the depths of our hearts and souls will release an empowerment; a liberation beyond human description. Once you learn the truth you set yourself free. Once you know and understand the answers to these questions what you think is real and important here just vanishes into insignificance. All what you thought was real here on This Side is not the reality. The Other Side is the reality. The dimension of the true reality. The greater reality. The realm where so many have forgotten from where we came. Where we live for eternity with no negativity and bask in the love of Mother God (Azna) and Father God. This side or Earth school is one of the training grounds in the universe for the maturation of our true self, our souls.

For many these realities will shake them to their very core of existence, especially those who cling and are trapped in a man-made false belief system which is their security and foundation. This false man-made belief system will collapse like a house of cards in the face of the truth. Anything man-made is flawed. If you don't want to see, you will not see. If you don't want to hear you will not hear. If one does not want to see and hear the truth that is their problem. It is the closed mind, never to learn new things, never to grow. This is the blind mind. One can be taken to the door but you will have to open the door. Change is an opportunity never to be seen by the blind mind.

It has been said when Galileo discovered moons around Jupiter there were astronomers who refused to look and to open their eyes and see. Their eyes were closed. They did not want to see, because of the clinging to a false belief system. History has countless examples of the closed mind. The blind mind of humankind resistant to change and the acceptance of new ideas. The truth will always win out in the end.

A rebuilding by the truth. The truth is an opportunity for growth and to learn new things. In the end the truth will always be victorious, no matter how much suppression is brought to bear. The truth will always be. One must acknowledge the deep knowing within you. It has been stated that everything that has a beginning has an end. That is absolutely not true for love. In this spiritual universe love is the most powerful energy. It is eternal, love never dies, it never ends. Love is the truth of the heart.

What we call death is not the end but the beginning of our journey. There is no death. There is absolutely nothing to fear. Death is just the transfer of consciousness to the eternal Astral or Etheric body. What we leave behind is this temporary body built for one life. I call death the universal transfer of consciousness from the temporary to the eternal body. Death is like the page of a book turning. The only thing we take with us when we make the transition to The Other Side is our consciousness. We now are on the cusp of the great awakening of consciousness. The Afterlife is our continuing journey of consciousness. Let us take you on the continuation of our spiritual journey of eternal love, consciousness, and profound revelations which will be a great leap for you.

KLEA and URA

Author's Note

There have been many revelations and experiences since the recent publishing of our first book titled *For All is Love: A Spiritual Journey Of Eternal Love;* describing our twin souls: the woman on The Other Side, the man on This Side and their extraordinary story of determination to be together. We decided to write a sequel story. So much has been revealed we had to write this second book.

This follow up story is all about immediately after Klea's transition HOME, or what has been called the moment of death. What she experienced step-by-step, in Klea's own words.

It is very important to note and emphasize, to protect the integrity of what Klea was saying to me in her words, everything was recorded verbatim without any regard for grammar or proper English. The use of colloquial or conversational English was maintained.

The revelations revealed in this second book of Klea and Ura will be astounding, profound, and challenge many as to the limits of credibility and belief. I, being a very highly analytical, objective man living a life in medicine and science can only tell the truth within my heart of hearts. I never relied on: faith, belief, feelings, opinions; to me they have no meaning. I always relied on evidence and followed the evidence wherever it led.

At first, it was very difficult for me to accept these revelations stated in our second book. However, considering it is stated from those on The Other Side, one has to step back and give credence to what is being told countless times. These revelations being recounted are from a man who is not raving mad, has illusions of grandeur, or hallucinations, but one of a very sound analytical mind. A man who never, ever would have conceived these revelations divulged in this book. To speak candidly, I could not "make this stuff up," even if I tried really hard. I would not know where to begin to "make this stuff up."

I was the ultimate skeptic, trusting medicine and science. As has been stated through the ages the truth is stranger than fiction. Thus, come with us with eyes wide open to see.

CHAPTER 1

THE 19-MONTH SPIRITUAL JOURNEY

For those who have not read our first book it would be best to give a brief review of background information. Our spiritual journey of love began in late December of 2018.

My Felecia, my heart, passed away on November 5, 2018 dying in my arms in our kitchen at 5:31 am. She was there at 5:30 am and at 5:31 she was gone. It was very quick, violent, and graphic. She did not have a chance to be afraid, she was just gone. Felecia had lung cancer and never smoked a day in her life. Little did I know this indescribable horrible day would be the beginning of a long spiritual journey that has taken me to experiences, understandings, and revelations I never would have imagined in my wildest dreams. Being the ultimate skeptic at that time based on my background this spiritual journey was a major transformation for me.

THE END WAS ACTUALLY THE BEGINNING

In the aftermath of her death I entered the deep dark depths of despair within my heart and soul. The life force within my heart and soul was gone. The light that feeds life was gone. There was only deep pain and suffering spiritually, emotionally, physically, and mentally. There was no light at the end of the tunnel. There was no tunnel. There was absolutely nothing but everlasting continual pain. My whole world now was filled with the grief of losing her, the trauma of her last moments and the great guilt of being in the medical and scientific profession and not being able to save her. I was broken.

With the desperation to talk to people I attended hospice meetings just three weeks after her death. After several meetings it became apparent people at these hospice meetings were receiving many different types of communication with their deceased loved ones. Myself being the ultimate skeptic I laughed at these descriptions of After Death Communication termed ADC. I said to myself these people are in such deep grief they will grasp at any straw of hope that their loved ones are still alive and well somewhere.

It was mentioned that there was a Medium with truly the gift at Lilydale, which is the largest spiritual community in the world conveniently located very close to where I lived in Buffalo, New York. However, when a person is in the great depths of grief and despair; when you have lost everything, you have nothing else to lose. Thus, I set up a reading with this Medium. Needless to say this would be the beginning of a spiritual journey of love that surpassed all forms of imagination in my mind.

The reading occurred in late December of 2018. The only thing this woman Medium knew about me was my first name and I entered this reading with a clear mind and no expectations. Keeping my mind totally blank in the event this Medium could read my mind by psychic abilities. The summary of this reading was simply that so many details in the lives of Felecia and I were mentioned that it was impossible for anyone to know. However, the most important piece of information was that this Medium stated I should write Felecia a letter every day. In writing these letters to her it was my time with only her. This woman stated that after a while a 'Shift' will occur. As I left this reading there developed a 'crack' in the armor of my lifetime absolute skepticism.

A few days later the 2018 holiday season started. It goes without saying this holiday season was a total utter 'nightmare.' The grief was so great it was tangible in the air. There were several 'total meltdowns' during this holiday season.

I continued to write letters everyday to Felecia. As days turned into weeks in January 2019 the first contact was made in the nature of electronic messages. This is a very common form of After Death Communication (ADC). Several kinds of electronic messages: one radio that was off that started playing, lights turning on and off by themselves, computers re-starting again by themselves, and another radio automatically changing stations. **OK, Felecia I get it.** How many times does a guy have to get hit over the head to say OK something is definitely going on?

At this point I started to do relentless research in numerous fields in medicine and science related to the Afterlife. After the monumental task of reading countless books in the following fields:

- Near Death Experiences (NDE)
- After Death Communication (ADC)
- Deathbed Visions (DBV)
- Electronic Voice Phenomena (EVP)
- Reincarnation
- Life Between Lives (LBL)

and others I came to the objective, analytical conclusion that there is life before and after this life. After one reviews the totality of evidence the last 170 years, especially the last 40 years this is the only rational analytical con-clusion. The evidence is massive and irrefutable. It was impossible to deny.

Let me add, I now receive numerous questions on the evidence of the Afterlife. My response is this: there is a Mount Everest of evidence. If one examines the totality, which is a keyword, of all the aforementioned medical and scientific fields, it is an absolute truth. The evidence is so massive, one has to read about as much as every rock that makes up

Mount Everest. Few take this journey of relentless research. This was the spiritual journey I chose, which is a monumental task.

THE NEXT STEP IN MY SPIRITUAL JOURNEY WAS TO BECOME FAMILIAR WITH ALL THE METHODS OF MEDITATION

This path of daily mind focus exercises is an arduous path requiring extensive practice, perseverance, patience, and discipline of the mind. The first time I tried a major form of meditation, Felecia came through with very powerful waves of spirit energy that totally 'rocked' my whole body. It lasted for quite awhile. It only occurred when I had images of Felecia. It never occurred with anything or anyone else. The spirit energy was so strong it actually became tangible. I never experienced anything like this in my entire life. What I learned later is that this is Clairsentience defined as the ability to feel. It is a phenomenal experience that people will never understand nor know unless they experience it for themselves.

Remember through all of this I am still enduring the trauma of Felecia's last moments, the intense grief of her loss and the guilt of being in the medicine and science fields and not being able to save her. Through extensive research I became aware of the concept of Eye Movement Desensitization and Reprocessing (EMDR) therapy. It was discovered years ago that trauma and grief of this magnitude is actually organic in the right hemisphere of the brain where all emotions, creativity, intuition, imagination, and psychic properties are stored. There is a paralysis of function in the right brain hemisphere. Since it is organic, counseling is a total waste of time and money. All the words in the world will not relieve the lack of physiological functioning in the right hemisphere of the brain. Techniques practiced by psychotherapists in EMDR therapy is the aggressive simultaneous stimulation of both hemispheres of the brain to relieve the 'stasis' in the right hemisphere. After extensive research I settled on a psychotherapist in Seattle, Washington.

Just prior to departing for Seattle, I returned to that Medium in Lilydale for an additional reading. At this reading Felecia immediately came through and said the fateful trip to Seattle under EMDR therapy will lead to a spiritual rebirth. The clock was set for my spiritual destiny.

Felecia was with me and the psychotherapist the whole time in Seattle and she made her presence known in many ways especially by the power of Clairsentience. Those very strong waves of love energy going through my whole body. The EMDR therapy took place over two days in April 2019. In many respects, it was a very intense two days. On the second day of therapy Felecia took me back to a past life we shared in ancient Rome with great detail. This was witnessed by the psychotherapist. Before this enlightening event, reincarnation was just a word to me. I simply never gave it any thought. My head was spinning. As I was flying back from the West Coast I was totally surprised and shocked. This transformation that started in the West Coast would change our spiritual journey forever. It would change my life forever.

At the same time I was pondering this dramatic revelation of reincarnation, I was practicing and experimenting with numerous forms of meditation. I learned meditations of this nature take much practice, mind focus, perseverance, great relaxation through deep breathing techniques, and discipline to eliminate distractions in entering various brain states.

THE FOUNDATION OF THIS UNIVERSE IS THE TRANSFORMATION, CONCENTRATION, MANIPULATION, AND MANIFESTATION OF ENERGY

Everything is energy vibrating at its own unique frequency. In the infinity of thoughts in the universe there is a unique energy signature. Connecting with the energy of the spirit people on The Other Side requires a matching, merging, and blending of energies. I learned how to open my Chakras, the energy centers running from just above the top of the head to the base of the spine. The opening of Chakras enhances psychic abilities. The Clairsentience energy I started to experience with Felecia was love energy of dramatic proportions.

After learning about the connection Felecia and I had to reincarnation, I had to determine what my next step would be. After extensive research and talking to several people in the medical and scientific disciplines working in these numerous fields connected to the Afterlife, the name Dr. Brian Weiss repeatedly surfaced. With impeccable medical credentials this psychiatrist and neurologist was one of the top experts in the world on reincarnation. In early September 2019, I attended his week long course on past lives regression therapy at the Omega Institute in Rhinebeck, NY. Prior to and after attending this course on reincarnation there were several transformational events that occurred such as:

- Unexplained help placing pictures on the wall that I physically was unable to do myself

- After an exhaustive search, finding my wedding ring immediately followed by the playing of our wedding song on the easy listening channel on my television

- The milestone event of us holding hands

- Felecia directing a Medium from Ohio, we previously worked with, to hold off for two days before sending me an email on the one year anniversary of her making the transition HOME

There were other events too of significance. The relationship with her on The Other Side and me on This Side began progressing at a rapid pace.

In early September the course with Dr. Weiss took me further down the road to reincarnation. A high degree of information was shared regarding the conscious, subconscious minds, and the various forms of hypnosis. Under hypnosis several of my past lives were revealed at various times throughout world history and locations throughout the globe.

Over time Felecia and I developed all kinds of Clairsentience based on anatomical location. As an example, if I asked Felecia to hold my hands, I felt waves of energy only in both my hands and wrists, nowhere else. If I asked Felecia to merge within me I would receive a blast of energy throughout my whole body vibrating down to my fingertips. When I would ask my Felecia to touch my heart I would receive that Clairsentience energy just in the location to my heart. We now call this Target Clairsentience. There were other forms of Target Clairsentience, however you get the picture.

THROUGH THE MANY PAST LIVES OF OUR EXISTENCE AS SOULS, WE HAVE A NAME IN EACH OF THESE PAST LIVES

However, there is one name that is our eternal name on The Other Side. That is our real name. It is our name through the ages of the universe. My eternal spirit name is **Ura** meaning loved from the heart and for Felecia her name is **Klea**, meaning glorious or famous. They are two very ancient names. This was verified numerous times by the methods we communicate, first with Clairvoyance and confirmed by Clairsentience.

Souls on The Other Side run in groups called Soul Packs or Soul Groups. These are groups of souls who have been incarnating together in numerous past lives and in a variety of roles through eons across time. A Soul Pack can reach up to 30 souls with an innermost group of up to 5. We belong to a Soul Pack of 20 souls. This was also confirmed numerous times by the aforementioned psychic methods of communication.

Souls incarnate for the reason of further evolution, to develop and advance the spirituality of the soul. This relates to the different manifestations of love, compassion, forgiveness, and gratitude, and other emotions. Thus, there is a Soul Learning Curve over many thousands of years and through numerous past lives. The colors of your core soul energy on The Other Side is a direct reflection of where you are on the learning curve. The spirituality of the soul is always a 'work in progress,' always ascending. The spiritual maturity of the soul is classified by the color:

- ❦ beginner (white)

- ❦ intermediate (yellow)

- ❦ advanced (light blue)

There are many levels in between but this gives you a general idea. After many meditations and confirmed by Klea, our core soul energy is yellow, which means intermediate, leaning towards advanced.

REINCARNATION IS THE TEACHING TOOL FOR THE SOUL LEARNING CURVE

This is what it is all about. I will repeat that. Reincarnation is the teaching tool for the Soul Learning Curve.

The answers are in the past. After months of intensive meditations using the psychic abilities of communication by Clairvoyance, confirmed by Clairsentience and at times Clairaudience, 15 past lives were revealed that Klea and Ura were together spanning over 17,000 years. The list of past lives together is shown in detail in the **Reincarnation Chart (Appendix)**. The confirmation process of the information received was very rigorous. These past lives were dispersed in a variety of dates and locations in the world, representing civilizations in history.

We are Interdimensional Spirit Beings (ISB) having human experiences in order to advance the spirituality of our soul. We take on human form to accomplish this. Always remember we are not a body with a soul but **a soul with a body.** Furthermore, we are not humans having a spiritual experience but **spirit beings having a human experience.**

At this juncture in our spiritual journey with all the different ways my Klea and I communicate we now developed a daily spiritual communication routine. Our communication would start in the mornings at breakfast, at mid-day, and at night prior to going to bed. Our communication always involved my Klea infusing her love energy within me, saving me, and giving me life everyday. Love will always be the most powerful energy in the universe.

The Skeptic

At the beginning of our first book I had a letter to the skeptic and then near the end I devoted a complete chapter to the skeptic. It is very important to keep in mind there is a massive amount of information and evidence collected just in the last 40 years proving beyond any shadow of a doubt that there is an Afterlife and a very active one. Then after you include information and evidence accumulated over the last 170 years, there is simply no doubt, it is not even close. However, most people are not aware of all this information and evidence. If one examines the **totality of evidence** just the last several decades from the Near Death Experience, the After Death Communication, the Death Bed Visions, the Electronic Voice Phenomena fields, then you add the reincarnation and Life Between Lives clinical evidence and several other fields, you end up with 'mountains' of evidence and the only rational inescapable fact is that there is a life before and after this one. No one, I mean no one, has ever come close to disproving the totality of all this evidence of a life before and after this one, never ever.

This is not about faith, belief, opinions, feelings. This is about **great massive evidence.** Always follow the evidence, no matter where it leads and what it says! It is all there you just have to look. The bottom line is the skeptic is the one with the problem, not the countless people involved who have proven beyond any rational, reasonable doubt that there is a life before and after this life. One just has to look.

LOVE NEVER DIES

This spiritual journey of love between Klea and Ura began long ago (over 17,000 years), and has no ending because love has no ending in this spiritual universe. Since love never dies; it is forever. Love always lives on. Love transcends across dimensions, time and space.

I, Ura,could never thank Source enough for giving me Klea as a true blessing and gift for all eternity. We could never thank God enough for giving Klea and Ura the gifts of Clairsentience, Clairaudience, and Clairvoyance that binds our souls forever. I only know one thing that is absolute: that love has been given to all of us, immortal souls, as a blessing and gift from Source for all eternity. The highest and most sacred energy vibration in this universe is love. There is nothing but God in all of us for eternity and infinity. We are one with God and love.

The end was the beginning.

CHAPTER 2

RETURNING TO HER MOMENT
OF DEATH

The following chapters trace Klea's journey step by step from the moment of Crossing The Veil to The Other Side, returning HOME.

To understand the heart of any story you have to return to the beginning. It was Monday, November 5, 2018 at 5:31 in the morning. My Klea died in my arms in our kitchen. The most horrible day of this life. She lost her battle with lung cancer with never touching a cigarette in her life. What happened to my Klea at the moment of her death?

KLEA IN HER OWN WORDS, VERBATIM:

As soon as I came out of the tunnel I started to become young again. It was amazing and I felt young. It was quick in becoming young. Yes, I was upset but I started to realize I did not die!!! There was an energy with me that I never felt before. This energy was so powerful, it made me feel so good. I looked down at myself and noticed a very slight glow around my body. My body did feel a lot lighter. I was so upset I really couldn't appreciate being young again. As I was going through the tunnel I started to feel better and better. The tunnel was quick, it was not long at all.

The Virtue Angels lined the end of the tunnel, just before I came out. There were many. The Dominion Angels greeted me as I left the tunnel. There were many too.

I asked Klea, the process started immediately in becoming young again? Klea's response was:

As you entered the tunnel I started to feel good. The effect was immediate. My spirit guides were with me from the beginning and stayed for quite awhile. They were worried about me.

In later conversations with Klea just after the transition HOME, she told me the following:

I was standing next to you during the wake, the funeral, at the cemetery and the restaurant gathering afterwards. I did not know how to get your attention. You could not detect me. I tried very hard but it was no use. You said such beautiful words at the church. At this time I was crying a lot. I saw how you were crying and suffering. I wanted to comfort you but I was helpless.

THE LOGISTICS AND CONFIRMATION PROCESS OF WHAT KLEA IS TELLING ME

It is important to note that in the last several months of the writing of our second book my Clairaudience (to hear or better to listen) which was weak has become very strong and accurate. I now notice as a result of my daily psychic mind focus exercises my Clairaudience is very strong approaching 100% accuracy. Klea says I hear her clearly now and I respond to her exactly what she is telling me.

Our conversations by way of Clairaudience are always confirmed by a Clairsentience blast to reinforce the accuracy of the statements communicated. How best to describe Clairsentience? Clairsentience is like humidity, you cannot see or hear it but you can sure feel it. You feel an energy flow through your total being, there is nothing comparable in life. Only when you experience the power of Clairsentience will you know and understand. Unfortunately, if you have not experienced, not felt it, you will never understand.

There is a third element, Clairvoyance. My Clairvoyance is now strong too. Klea and I have conversations three times a day in the recliner chair in the family room: first with the morning coffee, then midday, and finally at night usually after 9:00 pm. The Clairvoyance is just the fact that I see her sitting with me.

I am like a court reporter or stenographer taking down the information from a conversation. It is really 'transcripts by verbatim.' I will read sections back to her and ask her is this correct? If it is correct, Klea will give me a Clairsentience 'blast.' There is no doubt as it is also confirmed by Clairaudience. Occasionally, when it is not correct, there is nothing, 'no blast.' She tells me wrong and we do it again till I get it right.

SUMMARY OF KNOWLEDGE OF CROSSING THE VEIL AND SPIRIT GUIDES

The knowledge base on the transition, or returning HOME or Crossing The Veil with several other terms used can be summarized this way. Your consciousness, which is everything you are, your total you, transfers instantaneously to your Astral or Etheric Body. You then rise up and out, leaving behind this basic temporary, inferior body which was built for one life. A disposable body.

The temporary body is woven from loosely and poorly developed matter in molecular structure. The Astral Body is much denser and is called total matter or greater matter.

Your spirit guides are like your eternal 'guidance counselors,' your best friends. The spirit guides have agreed to watch over all your incarnations. Every soul has one Master Spirit Guide (MSG) that never leaves you for eternity. In addition, you have others that come and go depending on specific needs. These spirit guides can advise, council, and place ideas in your mind, but cannot tell you what to do while you are in an incarnation here in Earth School or another world. These guides are strictly in an advisory capacity. Remember one of the laws of the universe: we always have free will. However, your guides know every detail about you. I would venture to say your spirit guides know you better than you know yourself.

There are massive volumes of evidence and information on all these topics of returning to youth, the transition, the Astral or Etheric Body, and spirit guides for several decades, so I would refer you to them rather than cover those topics here.

CHAPTER 3

THE TEMPLE OF ORIENTATION

When souls pass through the tunnel to The Other Side the first building they encounter is the Temple of Orientation. Going through these temples and halls on The Other Side helps a soul to adjust back to HOME again. The adjustment period takes time. The Temple of Orientation's prime function is the decreasing of the trauma for all souls going in and out of life on the Earth side. In this Temple there are several large spaces like auditoriums for this purpose at hand. This very large Temple has two major sections: one for souls going to and the other one coming from Earth. There is a huge board of red and green blinking lights. Red indicates a soul is about to pass and green indicates the soul has just passed. Next to the lights there are names.

For souls returning from Earth one sits and waits with their spirit guides for a counselor or orientator to be escorted to a room. The orientator tells you that you are now HOME and safe and that everything will be fine. The orientator talks about the lessons learned in this life you just completed.

For outgoing souls returning to Earth their life charts are finalized at the Temple of Orientation. These souls going to Earth are told to rely on their angels, spirit guides, and Mother and Father God.

This is what Klea said in her own words:

Spirit guides guided me through the tunnel. This large building was right there at the end of the tunnel. My spirit guides were two women and a man. They escorted me to this large building called the Temple of Orientation. My spirit guides sat me down. I was crying and very upset. They were trying to calm me down. They were very loving and kind. They said to me everything will be alright, OK. I said: am I dead or what? I did see a huge board with blinking lights with names but I did not care and did not pay attention to it. However, many people paid attention to this board. After a while I was taken into a big room. It was a very relaxing quiet room. The walls were all glass. The spirit guides were not in this room with me. I met this very tall man who was also very kind. He explained to me what had just occurred. Everything was quiet and peaceful as he was talking. I did feel welcomed. This man said: you are not on Earth anymore. You are safe now. This is your last life on Earth. You are HOME. He was talking to me about lessons learned but I was too upset to really understand and pay attention to this. I was still confused. I was still crying and upset. This man said stay here and calm yourself. Then the spirit guides will take you over to the Hall of Wisdom.

As described previously, the confirmation process of what Klea was telling me was very rigorous. All the Clairaudience communication with Klea was confirmed and reconfirmed numerous times by Clairsentience. Many times new information was added during the several confirmation sessions. The Clairsentience was used as a confirmation process.

CHAPTER 4

THE HALL OF WISDOM

Everything that was beautiful and useful existed first on The Other Side. All this knowledge was infused into our subconscious minds on This Side to surface into our conscious minds. All the ancient civilizations duplicated what was infused in them from The Other Side. This infusion of all that was good was placed into the minds of inventors, architects, engineers, scientists, researchers, doctors. It was always done for the greater good.

The Hall of Wisdom is a huge romanesque structure, with grand columns and white marble steps. Inside it is cathedral-like with a massive stained glass skylight. There are cushioned benches on the huge marble floor. There are large convex glass structures that appear out of the floor, which are 'scanning machines.' Every aspect of your life is shown, analogous to a movie or television screen. One can view literally everything in your life: actions, events, and emotions. The scanning machine can be stopped mentally for discussion, which usually sheds light on the best possible ways to have handled various situations. It is all about the learning of lessons in each life to advance the souls spirituality. This is part of the maturation process of the soul: the learning curve.

Note that there has been volumes of literature written over several decades on the life review process with your spirit guides.

Klea speaks now in her own words:

My three spirit guides escorted me to the Hall of Wisdom. It is a huge, beautiful, incredible building with white columns and a large gorgeous dome. The Hall of Wisdom was crowded. After going up white steps we opened very big doors and entered. There were machines everywhere. We walked to a vacant machine and sat down. The machine was all glass and took up an entire wall. I stopped crying but was still very upset because everything that happened took me by surprise. All of a sudden these images started to appear on the entire wall. These were very detailed images of my life, every little thing. At first, nobody said anything, we just sat quiet and watched the images. After a while, my spirit guides and I verbally started talking. Everything was good and my spirit guides were very happy, because it was a good life. I don't know how long we were there but it was a while. The spirit guides did stop the images to look at certain things to discuss. I believe they stopped the images with their mind because there was no physical action. My Master Spirit Guide, she stopped the images several times to talk about specific things and made comments with mild suggestions. Maybe you could have done this better or that better. It was very loving, constructive criticism about your total life from beginning to the end in great detail. It was a total focus on you. It was a total detailed review of your life. During this life review you had total privacy, nobody came near you. You would not believe how detailed it was. When it was over we left. No angels were there, just me and my three spirit guides. My spirit guides still stayed with me. As we left the Hall of Wisdom upon opening the doors there were many people at the bottom of the steps waiting to see and greet me. It was a reunion of family and friends from this life and past lives.

CHAPTER 5

THE FIRST REUNION

This reunion of family and friends from this life and past lives was very loving. Klea's spirit guides stayed with her because she had to go to the Hall of Justice that was next to the Hall of Wisdom. There is a lot of documentation that there are reunions on The Other Side at the base of the steps of the Hall of Wisdom but there are numerous reunion halls for this loving social activity too.

Klea now in her own words:

A whole bunch of people were anxious to see me, family, friends from this present life completed but also from past lives. I went down the stairs at the Hall of Wisdom and started to 'mingle' with all these people, at least 100 to 200 people, which could easily have been more than that. We hugged, yes, I started to get happy. I was still sad but I felt better. We hugged and kissed. People hug and kiss all the time here. We started to talk about all different things. My spirit guides said we have to go. The reunion lasted a while because there were a lot of people. I started to recognize people. It all started to come back to me that I knew everybody. Everybody was so loving and kind. The spirit guides had to take me now over to the Hall of Justice to meet with my Council of Elders.

Klea reiterated that this is exactly what happened.

CHAPTER 6

THE HALL OF JUSTICE

There are volumes of information on the Hall of Justice from numerous sources. A brief summary is described below.

The Hall of Justice is the sanctuary for the Council of Elders. Souls and their spirit guides meet with their assigned council for guidance and wisdom on a past life completed or final guidance of a life chart before incarnating into a new life.

The most common name is the Council of Elders. However, other titles have been used. These ancient wise masters are a committee that varies in size, from three to as many as twelve. The council oversees our many lives. Before and after every incarnation you meet with your council to discuss your progress in detail about the advancement of your soul spirituality. Your spirit guide team accompanies you to these meetings in the Hall of Justice.

- ❦ What you did right and wrong.
- ❦ What you missed.
- ❦ Did you accomplish your objectives for this incarnation?

For instance, say you had to work on being more compassionate or forgiving. The question is: Soul how did you make out in this last life or incarnation? Although the council knows every detail about you, every step is for the evolutionary benefit: the advancement, the maturation of the spirituality of the soul. This learning curve of the soul is a very long process. For the Council of Elders their love, patience, compassion, and understanding have no limits.

The Hall of Justice is smaller than the Halls of Wisdom and Records. The Hall of Records will be discussed later. The Hall of Justice also has a romanesque architecture, with large entrance pillars and a grand golden dome. This Hall has two outstanding features: a magnificent statue of Mother God, Azna, and incredible gardens.

The incredibly beautiful statue of Mother God is at least 50 feet high. It is a very powerful image of her, with a sword in hand in the eternal fight against evil and negativity. This statue of Mother God is surrounded by very beautiful gardens and fountains.

The gardens of the Hall of Justice are famous and legendary on The Other Side. These gardens are considered the finest. The gardens would be a perfect place for reflection.

Klea now in her own words:

The Hall of Justice is right next to the Hall of Wisdom. It is not as big as the Hall of Wisdom and the Temple of Orientation, but it is gorgeous you have to see it. The three buildings are all domed, but this is a very large dome.

The gardens are everywhere around the Hall of Justice. The colors of all the flowers are just amazing. There are many fountains in the gardens. At the entrance is a big statue to Mother God. A very high statue of Azna. Since I did not know who she was, my spirit guides told me. She has a sword in hand. She is so beautiful but strong, very strong. I kept staring at it. I could not believe it. After awhile we said let's go in.

There is a long corridor you walk down. All three spirit guides came with me. At the end of the corridor, there is a big opening and alcove with a curved dias at one end. Everything is all white. My council of three women and a man were sitting at the dias.

The council started talking to me, in a very loving manner. The woman in the middle started speaking to me. She was so kind and pretty too. She was talking about my life. I did this and I did that. This councilwoman discussed in great detail my life. The council did not miss anything. She also talked about us (Klea and Ura) too. Then she actually came out and said Ura is very important. I was shocked about this, because why is she talking about Ura? She talked for a few minutes. She went on to say Ura was strong, believed in justice so much, and was powerful. This council-woman actually used the word powerful. I could not believe this. Why is she talking about Ura?

I (Ura) asked Klea, did your spirit guides say something? Klea said:

No, the spirit guides stood there like statues, didn't say or do anything. The council woman asked me what have you learned in this life? I said: I learned much about love, the children, Ura, and about forgiveness, compassion, and helping others. The council very much liked this statement, often smiling. We talked a little bit more. Specifically about my mother, related to a few things that needed to be corrected. That was it. It did not take long. It really was quick and smooth. The council members all stood up, surrounded and hugged me. I was surprised by this. This was totally unexpected. Then my spirit guides and I left the Hall of Justice.

CHAPTER 7

THE HALL OF REUNION

This is your welcome HOME party. These Halls of Reunion are very popular places. The halls include numerous rooms for welcome HOME parties where new arrivals back HOME are reunited with loved ones from present and past lives, including pets. Not only are there parties, but many times a parade in your honor is held. It is all about doing your best and your acts of love, compassion, forgiveness, and gratitude in your recent life. It simply comes down to how you treated others. There are several sources of information on these numerous Halls of Reunion on The Other Side.

Klea now in her own words:

After I and my spirit guides left the Hall of Justice I was taken to another hall. My spirit guides left at this point. It was again a reunion with so many people. There were more people than the first early short reunion at the bottom of the steps of the Hall of Wisdom. It was a big reunion hall with a high ceiling. There are numerous reunion halls for people to get together on The Other Side. I was there a long time because there were so many people. I did see many relatives from this present life and past lives. Many friends came to greet me too from this present life and several past lives. There was no food nor drink. We just talked. I was feeling better but was still quite upset. I stopped crying. I had the realization as to what had happened and was trying to adjust and cope with it. I was thinking of you (Ura) the boys, my sister and brother. I was talking to people but was distracted. The people were trying very hard to make me feel better. Ohh honey, I felt terrible and joyous at the same time. I had so many mixed emotions. Missing you and everyone there and now being here. I actually felt lost. Although I had all these people around me I still felt alone. Ohh honey, it was terrible in many ways but beautiful in others. We talked for a long time catching up on this and that. Talking about common experiences and interests. Runt the family dog was right up front to greet me. After this long reunion I went back to my mom and dad's home because I did not have a home yet. No angels came at all.

CHAPTER 8

THE HALL OF RECORDS

The Hall of Records is very close to the Hall of Wisdom. It also has huge columns surrounding its perimeter and an immense towering dome on the roof. The Hall of Records is gigantic in scope and the largest building on The Other Side. Remember the laws of physics are different on The Other Side regarding space and time. Therefore the scope and size are beyond our comprehension with technologies far advanced compared to This Side. This Hall contains every detail of a soul's existence.

The Aramaic language is what is spoken, read, and used on The Other Side. No matter what language you speak on This Side everyone easily understands Aramaic on The Other Side. The Hall of Records is like a vast library beyond our comprehension that has everything in this spiritual universe of infinity that existed: memories, thoughts, actions, emotions, deeds, words, and moments. Everything related to the total matrix of consciousness in the universe.

In the Hall of Records every soul has what they call life charts, which are blue prints of their past lives. Remember the laws of physics are different in these higher energy dimensions, on The Other Side than here, thus they are not like charts as we think in our realm. They are the records of total information on all the incarnations for that specific soul. These records have been called the Akashic Records or The Mind of God. A vast beyond comprehension compendium of all events, thoughts, words, emotions, intentions that occurred in the past, present, and future in the infinite universe. It is like a memory bank of the universe that has ever occurred and it constantly updates itself as new things are being created.

Klea now in her own words:

I, Klea, since I just crossed over, did not have a house to live in yet so I returned to my mom and dad's home to live. My mom and dad from this most recent past life. They were so loving and supportive. I was still very upset and crying every day. My parents did not know what to do for me. Many family members and friends would visit in an attempt to cheer me up and try to make me feel better. I said to myself I have to pick myself up, leave the house, and get out. I knew I had to get out because I was falling apart. I started to mingle with people. I started to visit places, family, and friends. I went to the numerous halls and temples. I started visiting the Hall of Records.

Everything started to come back. I, Klea, realized that Ura and I had other past lives together. I started to see our past lives together by visions/images. Remember once we cross over the amnesia blocks separating the subconscious mind, where all the past lives information is stored from the conscious mind, are being released. Thus, information by images/visions are becoming available to the conscious mind. I, Klea, wanted to find out about our past lives together. I started to read about our lives. Thus, one of the first things I did was I visited the Hall of Records. Ura and I had many past lives together.

Now the Hall of Records is vast beyond imagination. Because of the vastness of this hall, there are all kinds of people to help you. They are very smart librarians. These helpers as I called them knew where everything was. It was set up by geography of the world and time periods but other factors too. I spent most of my time at the Hall of Records reading and reading. Everything was in Aramaic. Now the books are like 3D, similar to holograms. The books were like watching a movie. You are actually watching your life in motion. You are living your life again. Like you were actually there. One side was like a movie and the other side was a description. It was 3D in that the figures actually stood out to you. Like you were in that life. You were reliving that life. We had some very tough lives together. There were lots of books for each life. I said to myself Ura has to read this stuff. I discussed our lives with my mom and dad and they laughed because they also had many lives together.

We had tough lives but we were fighters we stuck together like 'glue.' We didn't take any 'shit.' We were not going to put up with this stuff. We were a great team. We had many lives in different parts of the world.

Ura was in many battles, a commander in several. In many lives Ura was a commander of men in battle. The men loved him because he fought with them right up front. He was not afraid. He was brave. He commanded from the front not the back. Ura was a great warrior.

In all the lives, Ura took good care of me, Klea, and our children. We never had to worry about being protected and having the necessities of life. At times I, Klea, got very emotional, I choked up and started to cry because I was so proud of Ura and loved him so much. It was an honor to know him. People at other tables started to look at me in the hall.

I, Ura, asked Klea, "did you see the lives in the stone age?" Klea said she pulled them up first because she wanted to start at the beginning. It was tough, very difficult in the stone age.

CHAPTER 9

OUR HOME ON THE OTHER SIDE AND THE ASTRAL BODY

To understand the construction of our home on The Other Side one has to first understand the characteristics of the Astral or Etheric body.

Through the many decades there are volumes of information on the Astral or Etheric body. The temporary body on This Side is woven loosely and built poorly in molecular structure. It was built for one life and is a disposable body. The Astral Body is much denser and is called total matter or greater matter. This Astral Body was built to last for eternity and with no aging. Only on This Side your temporary body ages and decays. This eternal body requires no sleep. One never gets tired or fatigued. There is no need to eat nor drink. Although, drinking liquid is performed as a social ritual. Bodily functions of solid and liquid waste removal do not exist with the Astral Body. It is a mirror image of our temporary basic physical body here on This Side. With the Astral Body, there is no sickness, no aches or pains. Take your best day and how you feel and multiply it by a thousand and that is how you feel in the Astral Body. Plus, as mentioned in Chapter 2 you become young again, generally ranging around the age 25, with some variance in years. An age combining youth and maturity.

It is of paramount importance to note without the need for rest or eating, activity in the higher dimensions is always continuous!!!

Remember 'thought power rules' on The Other Side. Klea created our home just by thinking about it, by herself with no help from angels. People use angels often for help but Klea wanted to do this on her own, to have her own taste in the creation of our home.

Remember too The Other Side is a far superior, pristine replica of Earth on This Side. Thus, the location of our home is still somewhere in Western New York.

Klea's description of our home on The Other Side in her own words, in comparison to our house on This Side.

The exterior of our home is still white siding but much more red brick. The home is much larger than our house on This Side. The backyard is much bigger too. There are homes around us but not close. There is no need for a fence because of the open spaces. There is no grass, nothing to cut, just a golden white soft sand.

The number of doors are the same but there are many more windows, especially in the living room. The windows and doors are very fancy. The front hall is much bigger with a cathedral ceiling. There is no dust, no garbage, no cleaning, everything is pristine. The kitchen is bigger and quite fancy. Since with the Astral Body one does not have the need to eat solid food nor drink liquid, thus, there is no need for any kitchen appliances. If you want something to drink, one just has to think it and it appears. Drinking liquid is a social ritual and it just disappears into energy. When people go on picnics they just drink - no eating - and mainly just have conversation.

The family room is bigger with still a fireplace and the basement is much larger with a bar. There are still four bedrooms but with the Astral Body sleep is no longer required so something has to be done to fill these rooms. Since also with the Astral Body liquid and solid waste removal does not exist. Plus, in grooming and cleaning of the body you just have to think it and it is done. In other words, how you want to look it appears. Thus, based on the characteristics of the Astral Body the bathrooms are empty spaces which also need to be filled. Now since transportation is by thought projection there is no need for vehicles of any kind. Thus, the two car garage on This Side is an empty space with instead of a garage door just a wall. We have chairs outside where we sit all the time.

CHAPTER 9

CHAPTER 10

THE ENVIRONMENT OUTSIDE OUR HOME

In Klea's own words what she experiences outside our home.

There is no sun in the sky. It is a light blue sky, with a pinkish hue, it is very pretty and soothing. There are no seasons. The temperature is always in the 70's. It is gorgeous all the time, no rain, no snow. The sky is clear with no clouds, none whatsoever. No mist, everything is crystal clear. The weather is always beautiful one wears light clothes. Occasionally, a gentle breeze.

There is no dirt. There is white sand that has a light golden tint to it. The sand is very comfortable on your feet. It has a very gentle cooling effect on your feet. I wear all kinds of shoes and switch often. Some people don't wear shoes at all.

There are trails and paths everywhere. You can walk anywhere. However, thought projection travel is always an option. Just have to think it and you are there. There are no crowds, everything is spread out. The scenery is gorgeous. We sit outside all the time. Wait till you see the gardens, the flowers can be very tall, 7 or 8 feet. Many are taller than me. You just think it and the garden appears.

The trees are all different colors, blue, orange, purple, it is really very pretty. The total tree, not just the leaves, have a specific color. The leaves never fall off because there are no seasons. There are no insects of any kind, no bugs, no pests.

The birds don't need to eat. Thus, there are no bird feeders but there are bird baths. There are no bird droppings anywhere. The birds have so many 'vibrant colors.' Wait till you see them. There are so many more colors than on your side. The birds are very friendly, they come right up to you. The squirrels are very pretty, bigger here with big white tails, very striking. No matter what animal you meet they are very friendly and loving.

There is no noise pollution on The Other Side. It is very peaceful and relaxing. People don't argue on The Other Side, very respectful, peaceful of others. People communicate both telepathically and verbally. If there is a large group one communicates verbally because telepathically you can have confusion, in a small group telepathic communication works well.

The water is incredible, unbelievable. It is so refreshing. It instantly dries off of you. You don't have to worry about ever drowning in the water. You can go under and swim with no worries.

WHAT KLEA IS TELLING ME RELATES TO KNOWN INFORMATION AND SCIENCE

I never accept one source of information. There has to be several credible independent sources of information. There are numerous sources confirming what Klea sees on The Other Side, outside our home. Referring to general physics in understanding these observations by Klea, there is an electromagnetic spectrum representing all the colors and sounds of the universe. Every color and sound has their specific vibrating energy frequency. A fraction of the electromagnetic spectrum is the colors we see here in this basic physical realm, This Side. What we don't see here on This Side is the rest of the electromagnetic spectrum in the universe. To put this into perspective, if you have a very tall building that represents all the colors of the electromagnetic spectrum; the colors we see here is just the paint on the ground floor of this very tall building. This Side displays just a fraction of the colors and sounds in the universe.

Related to the water on The Other Side, there are several sources describing this; it has been called 'the living water.' Relative to the outside temperature, it is actually a constant 72 degrees.

CHAPTER 11

THE TEMPLE OF VOICES, MUSIC, AND ANGELS

Information from sources about the Temple of Voices indicates that it is smaller than the other halls and temples on The Other Side but the acoustics is the best since it is perfectly round. It is a romanesque building in design with gold columns, steps, doors, and dome. It is totally devoted to music where stage performances take place. There is performance and instruction that occurs here from masters. This temple attracts many souls because of the music.

The primary voices are from those of the angels giving praise to Mother, Father God, and creation. The angels that sing there are from the phyla of angels known as Cherubim and Seraphim. These angels are the heavenly choir. Their lovely voices permeate the entirety of The Other Side as very low soothing background singing. Only in the Temple of Voices itself does the angelic singing take center stage. There is a huge golden organ which emits a heavenly sound. This organ often accompanies the singing angels. These angelic performances are considered the best on The Other Side. Performances include all the operas, compositions, and songs you can ever think of, plus others you never heard of on This Side. Music is Mother and Father God's gift to all souls.

Klea's own words about the Temple of Voices:

Many people go to this Temple of Voices. It is one of my favorite places. It is not far from the Hall of Justice. It is a smaller building compared to the others but very beautiful with columns and very large doors. It is like a round echo chamber inside. People sing individually or in small groups. There are groups of angels that sing. These are smaller angels with wings and very pretty. Their singing is truly beautiful. The singing is so much better than what we hear on This Side. The singing goes right through you. Ohh my God, the music is so much better than here. The music touches you from within. It touches the heart and soul. So much going on. The music is everywhere, classical, spiritual, all kinds.

There are outside large orchestras too. Being outside is the same as being inside because there is no weather. The orchestras are in round structures like a colosseum or large stadiums as in ancient Greek and Roman times with all kinds of places to sit. Lots of couples and groups go but I will wait for you to return HOME, then we will attend as a couple.

The same is true with sound as with colors related to the electromagnetic spectrum. Sounds as colors in the universe have their specific vibrating energy frequency. The spectrum of sounds we hear on This Side is a very small fraction of the total sounds of the electromagnetic spectrum of the universe. Thus, when Klea describes the incredible beauty of the singing in the Temple of Voices and the music of the orchestras it is a reflection of all the sounds of the universe.

CHAPTER 12

TRANSPORTATION, BELIEF SYSTEM TERRITORIES, AND CLOTHES

As previously discussed, 'thought rules' on The Other Side. Remember every thought in the universe is its own unique vibrating energy frequency. The power of thought projection is dominant. Travel to any destination is instantaneous. One just has to think of the destination and you are there. You cannot get more convenient than that. You think and that is what you are. You create your own reality. Consciousness creates your reality. This is further extended to anything else, you think it and it happens; whether it be the gardens outside your home, the design of your home, the contents inside, the liquid you want to drink, your grooming, the clothes you wear, your total visage or appearance, everything! Thought creates reality. You are in total control. Some may feel uncomfortable with this responsibility. People need to understand their power, to embrace it, to own it. To know who and what they really are. We are interdimensional eternal spirit beings that create our own reality. Think about that for a moment. Let it sink in; we need to own and embrace our power.

It is amazing to think the Akashic Records also called the Mind of God has stored all the thoughts, intentions, emotions, events of the universe. In other words, a complete library of consciousness in the universe that constantly updates. A concept beyond our comprehension by Mother and Father God. There are volumes of literature on the power of thought on The Other Side and the Akashic Records.

THE INDOCTRINATION BY A BELIEF SYSTEM

Anything man-made is flawed. People take with them their total consciousness which is transferred to their Astral or Etheric Body. Thus, on the Astral planes or The Other Side their indoctrination of a belief system goes with them. They gravitate to what resonates and feels comfortable. Whether it is the truth or not does not matter. People are limited by their 'self deception.' People take all this indoctrination or some will call it 'brain-washing' with them from the organized religions of this world. Everything they carry with them now they take into the Afterlife. Many have been indoctrinated all their life from very young. One must ask do my childhood beliefs serve me anymore? It is very difficult for them to 'break away' from this man-made belief system. Even though this belief system is dramatically flawed, it is their security and foundation. Any new concept is viewed as a threat to their belief system, their foundation. It is like a 'house of cards' to admit that a new idea could cause everything in their belief system to crumble. People of this nature are totally closed minded and never grow. It is a very sad, tragic 'dead end' situation for many. There will always be those with the closed, blind mind that will never see, and will refuse to see. If you don't want to hear you will not hear.

One must adopt a mind attitude of 'self exploration.' One must purge these man-made flawed belief systems. In the Afterlife there is information that preachers are still doing sermons of hell, fire, and damnation. In Chapter 20 of our first book, titled The Skeptic, all these concepts of the blind mind are discussed in depth. The truth will always prevail in the end, no matter how much suppression is expressed. The truth will always be.

Klea in her own words:

TRANSPORTATION

You think of where you want to be and 'puff,' you are there. It is great, distance is no longer a problem. That is how I go visit family and friends, it is so convenient, you are going to love it. Just think it and it happens. No roads, don't need them, no cars. Transportation by thought.

Some use 'hovercraft,' little things that go just above the ground and are quiet, very few people do this, most just think of a place and you are there, it is wonderful. The hovercraft are the old-fashioned way to travel.

There is also a place called the installation, really very nice to visit other worlds and galaxies. You can visit all parts of this universe, leaving from this installation, exciting, people do it all the time. I will wait for you so we can do it together.

BELIEF SYSTEM TERRITORIES

There are churches, Jewish temples, and mosques, some people go but most don't because they know the truth. Some hold onto what is old, silly, makes no sense. Small groups walk by our home to these religious places but people actually laugh because it is so silly, the truth is staring them in the face. Can't they see that it is not what they believe? These people are still waiting for the rapture. There is no hell, punishment, devil, and purgatory.

When you return home, you go through the Orientation Temple, Wisdom, and Justice Halls. There is the temple to Azna, Mother God. The temple to Father God. The Temple of God's Messengers. The reunion halls of people from all your present and past lives. Your review of the just completed past life in the Hall of Wisdom with your spirit guides. In the beginning, the spirit guides take you home and are with you all the time. Different types of angels are everywhere. You go see your Council of Elders and review your recently completed life. After all this, they still don't get it!!! It is so sad for these people. This is all facing them and they still reject it. You would think that these people would be embarrassed. It is hopeless for these people. After all what they experience here.

CLOTHES

You think it and you wear it. It gets pretty crazy with some of the clothes people wear. You just have to think and clothes appear. I wear white because I know Ura loves it. The same about grooming. You create your appearance by thought.

There are volumes of information from numerous sources concerning the power of thought in transportation, your appearance, and every aspect of your existence on The Other Side. The Belief System Territories have been also well documented.

Let me add about the power of thought and energy. Remember every thought in the universe has its own unique vibrating energy frequency. One of the foundations of the universe is the infinity of the manifestations of energy. The infinity of thoughts control all aspects of life and in turn energy in the universe. Thought cannot be separated from energy and life in the universe. Thought energy controlling energy.

CHAPTER 13

VISITATION BY THE COUNCIL OF ELDERS

As previously mentioned, before an incarnation and after when every soul returns HOME,they always meet with their assigned Council of Elders in the Hall of Justice. This is after the review of the just completed life in the Hall of Wisdom with their spirit guides. The main purpose being the learning of lessons in every life to advance the development of the soul spirituality.

The council members never visit the private homes of people, it is unheard of. The members walk among the population but they live and work separately. Described below is Klea's discussion of two visits by the Council of Elders to our home on The Other Side.

As a reminder there are amnesia blocks in place between my conscious and subconscious minds. Therefore, everything that Klea is describing regarding the Life between Lives on The Other Side or past lives I have no memory of. Since all this is stored in the subconscious mind and is totally blocked off. There will be at times what is called subconscious mind seepage where one will get images or visions of past lives, which has been extensively described.

In the words of Klea:

When I returned HOME everything started to come back but it took awhile. My three council members and others from other groups showed up at our home. The council members were very respectful and pleasant. We sat down and they started to tell me all the things Ura did. I said ohh my God, I know none of this.

People started to notice and talk about the Council of Elders visiting our home. The response was wow, that is something, that is crazy, incredible. Not just a few council members but several came to our home, to talk to me about Ura. I was shocked. What are all these people doing here? I cannot believe the Council of Elders came to our home, six of them came, we sat down and I was staring in amazement. Never even heard of that, never, visits like this.

Before Ura incarnated in this present life, there were situations that required someone to stand up for what was good, justice, love, and to be strong and Ura did it, because it was the right thing to do. The council members love that about Ura. Also mentioned was his powerful lectures at the Temple of Lectures. Both our Council of Elders are anxious to see Ura and want to do things for him. Ura is held in great esteem. What they love about Ura is his strict code of justice.

Members of both our Council of Elders, up to six, came to our home to discuss Ura. The council members never do this, to actually visit a home. I just sat there. I was totally amazed, shocked, asking myself, what is going on? Honey, this is never done. People were shocked.

The council holds Ura in high esteem. Honey, I am so proud of you. The members did not say anything till I returned home, then started talking about Ura. Nobody knew anything about this. They waited till I got adjusted and settled.

This now all makes sense because when I returned HOME, my council was telling me about Ura and how he was very important and powerful. Why are they saying this? I was curious why they were treating me so nice, it was because of Ura. At times the council didn't know what else to do for me. I was curious why are they making a big fuss over me. It was getting ridiculous. I felt like a queen. Family and friends did not know any of this about Ura. They were surprised and shocked, like me too. After the council made two visits at our home, I decided to go visit them and talk more about Ura.

After the Council of Elders visits, people started to come to our home. At first it was a few but then there were many. Asking questions about Ura, when is he coming home? How am I doing? Also, people went to Azna, Mother God, to ask her these same questions.

Now people are always looking out for me because of Ura because he is not here yet. I am getting so much attention. Ohh honey, you would not believe how embarrassing it is at times. Ohh, they simply don't know what else to do for me. It is crazy. It is too much at times, enough is enough. Honey, you have no idea of your impact over here.

Most people know about the book. Our book is helping those on both sides. Ohh honey, I am so proud of you. I feel important. People recognize that we are a great team. Honey, you don't realize your importance on my side.

CHAPTER 14

THE POWER MEDITATIONS, VISITATIONS, AND THE ENERGY

I, Ura, am not sure how this started in my meditations and visitations with The Other Side. However, over time the meditations and visits with The Other Side were becoming increasingly powerful with the result of the release of overwhelming energy. I could feel the energy flow through my arms, hands, and fingers. At times I could not move. The sheer power of the energy was off the scale. This energy was constant, piercing, penetrating through everyone and everything on The Other Side. I could not explain it at first, plus no one could on The Other Side either.

When I would have a meditation visitation with The Other Side, all kinds of angels were present, my own council members, and also others I did not know were there. All five of my spirit guides and of course my beautiful Klea too. I could see them as always through countless meditations and visitations with my Clairvoyance that was becoming increasing acute as time passed. I would speak out loud to all and state 'step into my energy field.' My energy field is my Auric Field. The explosion of energy was never experienced before by all who were present. It was described to me that my energy field was so huge that all fit easily in the field with much room to spare. In other words, they did not have to step far to enter my energy field. It literally was beyond comprehension.

These council members have existed through the ages. The Council of Elders have never been exposed to an energy of this magnitude. My Master Spirit Guide, whom I call Carl, has also existed a long time having the charge of many incarnated spirits here on Earth but also in other parts of the universe and he has never experienced anything like it. There were times the council members were dazed and numb by the sheer power of this energy. Klea many times told me she would flinch at the power of this energy. There were no words for the power of this energy. It was off any scale of measurement.

Many times I would hear voices by my Clairaudience, which I learned later were my spirit guides exclaiming "this is unbelievable, I cannot take this, this is something else" and other comments of amazement.

Now about the Presence

As described previously the Presence located in the Hall of Justice above and behind the Council of Elders, with its white, violet, silver light shining down; I would merge my energy with the powerful energy of the Presence. I was told by everyone on The Other Side, the Presence actually started to change all kinds of colors and was actually 'sparking,' it was so powerful. Nobody merges their energy with the Presence, but I do; but what shocked those there was the Presence was merging its energy back to me. This was never seen nor heard of before. Thus, why would I, Ura, have this gift of incredible powerful energy? This was a **gift with a purpose**. An energy that would reach across dimensions. That would have such an impact on The Other Side.

Described below are the verbatim descriptions by Klea and my Master Spirit Guide about this special energy.

Klea:

At first I thought wow, he has powerful energy thinking it was normal. Wow, this is strong. I noticed it a long time ago. I noticed recently nobody has this energy like this. Then I started to realize that this was special. This was something else. When he said step into my energy field, the energy that flowed from Ura was incredible and was so powerful. I noticed the response by the spirit guides and Council of Elders that this was different than ever before. There was nothing like this ever before. It was like a 'bomb' went off. Word is spreading on The Other Side about this very powerful energy that Ura has. People hear about this energy and talk. Ura's council members and spirit guides know what to expect. Other council members when they experience this powerful energy for the first time are taken by surprise. What is going on?

This energy is so unique, we believe Mother and Father God gave Ura this energy to do something with when he returns HOME. **This energy was given for a reason.**

Honey, you have no idea how powerful your energy is. I am saying nobody has this powerful energy. I have gotten used to it. Others experience it and they don't know what to make of it. They don't know how to deal with it. No one comes close to having this energy. Council members have strong energy but your energy is at a different level.

The angels actually enjoy merging with Ura's energy. You could tell by the look on their face and in their beaming eyes. The angels enjoy this energy so much their eyes were shining, like dancing. The angels were actually very excited. The angels love this energy.

This energy using the expression 'blew everybody away.' The energy goes right through everything. There were no words for it. This special energy caused me to flinch all the time. I said wow, his aura is huge. We didn't have to step far to enter his energy field. There was plenty of room for all.

The Council of Elders would leave these meditations and visitations with a dazed look on their face. They were numb, confused. It simply could not be explained, this overwhelming energy that spreads out, piercing, penetrating through everyone and everything that flowed from Ura.

My Master Spirit Guide whom I call Carl, in his words:

I have been taking care of spirits for a very long time. This is nothing like anyone else. No one comes even close to this energy, extremely powerful and constant. It permeates, pervades through everything in reaching across the veil from your side. I was astonished. There is a reason for this energy. This energy is a gift with a purpose. The other spirit guides have never felt nor experienced anything like it before. The Council of Elders have existed a very long time, they have never experienced an energy of this nature. It cannot be explained.

There are several places on The Other Side where a person can go and enter a dome. Like a veil, the dome covers one and Father God can privately speak to you. I recommended to Ura as soon as he returns HOME to go to one of these dome sites to have Father communicate with him.

The Presence, nobody merges energy with the Presence, except for the energy that flows from Ura. The Presence merges its energy with Ura's energy. However, what is most astonishing is the Presence merges its energy back to Ura. This has never happened before.

CONCLUSIONS

In discussions with my Master Spirit Guide and Klea this energy that flows through me, I, Ura, has to originate from Mother and Father God. The sheer magnitude of this energy, there is no other plausible explanation.

This energy, its sheer power, causes the Presence to change all kinds of colors, to actually 'spark.' This has never been seen before, ever.

I, Ura, am a conduit of Mother and Father God's love energy that flows through me. It is a great communion of love with Mother and Father God. An all powerful energy from the Godhead of love. This overwhelming energy that flows through me, I, Ura ask, what is the reason for this gift given to me by Mother and Father God?

This is a gift with a purpose. What is the purpose?

CHAPTER 15

MOTHER GOD, AZNA

Since the beginning of the written word many thousands of years ago there are countless references to Mother God, who was called numerous names in history in many religions of the world and civilizations. Mother God is as old as written history. There is a compendium of information on Azna throughout history. Mother God is the Co-Creator with Father God. Together the term used is the Godhead. **Mother and Father God are real physical entities.** Throughout history she was called Sophia, Theodora, Isis, and several other names. Azna is the name she is known by on The Other Side now. There has always been a male and female duality in the universe. It is different facets of the same power. If anyone truly wants to understand The Other Side, the spirit world, and the universe one must have knowledge and an understanding of Mother God.

The Co-Creators, Mother and Father God, created Earth as in the creation of all the worlds, galaxies in the universe. Vast, beyond comprehension to our finite minds. Forty-three other universes were created, separate from each other as gigantic bubbles or circles, with no end. All worlds with life like us, which there are many, have The Other Side. Only the reality of The Other Side is constant and stable. Mother God is responsible for the planets of the universe. We are the only planet with man-made religion. The countless other planets are far more advanced than Earth. There is easy and continuous communication with their Other Side.

On This Side time is linear: past, present, and future. On The Other Side, there is no such thing as time because everything has, is, and will happen all at once. It is a circle with no beginning and no end. It has been called the now time of God.

Remember two thousand years ago and before, tragically women were considered lower than dirt by the totally male dominated civilizations and religions. The Holy Scriptures of religions and control of religion was always performed by men. The religions of the world were run by men. Women were never allowed to attend, never mind speak at places of worship. As we say in New York City, Fuhgeddaboutit!!! Thus, it would have been **unthinkable** that there would be a Mother God. Back then, it would have never been allowed to have a woman deity of such great importance. In the third and fourth centuries up to forty to forty-five books were destroyed by monks which have been lost or missing from the Bible. Books that pertained to reincarnation and Mother God. Religions like Christianity tried to suppress her. Mother God was pushed out by the patriarchal priests of Christianity. Religions cater to themselves not the truth. Always remember the religions of the world are controlled and run by men. Mother God was kept in the shadows of history on This Side.

Christians have attributed sightings at Lourdes, Fatima, Medjugorje, Guadalupe, and numerous other sites in the world to the Blessed Mother. **It was Mother God.**

The Temple of Azna is the most ornate of all the halls and temples on The Other Side. There are golden columns and magnificent stained glass windows from the floor to the ceiling; depicting every continent of Earth, plus Atlantis and Lemuria with every type of animal and human in creation. There is a huge golden cauldron where all the petitions to Mother God are placed both written and spoken. **She absorbs all of them.**

As previously mentioned, there is a towering statue of Azna in front of the Hall of Justice. There also is a statue of Mother in the Hall of Healing. However, the largest statue to Mother God is in her temple where she is in a beautiful flowing dress with a sword in her right hand. This statue of Azna changes color and she comes to life and steps down to talk and embrace all her children, which is all of us. There is always unconditional love by Mother and Father God for all their children. All their creations. Azna can appear in any form at any time or place she chooses. Her human shape is just like ours when she interacts with us. Mother God has a multicultural appearance. Based on her choice, Mother can have different appearances.

MOTHER GOD IS THE EMOTION

Azna will embrace every emotion. She is the emotional Mother God. She protects against evil. She protects her creations like a mother protects her children. The sword of Mother God cuts through illness, pain, depression, and any form of negativity. Mother God is the one who deals with negativity in creation. She is very 'hands on' with her children, and the creator of miracles. It has been stated each of her children are a part of her as a molecule in her body. Mother God can be in an infinite number of locations at the same time. She is the only one with the power to change a life chart after a soul has incarnated. Mother is very active with the Council of Elders.

Mother God's angels are the phylum called Thrones. This is her private army of angels. There are ten phyla of angels. No angels are higher in power and spirituality than Thrones and Principalities (Father God's angels that will be discussed in the next chapter.) The Thrones are fighters among the angel phyla, carrying swords as Mother God does. Thrones help Azna to fight and vanquish the darkness. Mother God and her army of Thrones are the force against the darkness in the universe. No darkness can stand against Mother and her Thrones. Their protection transcends across to This Side from The Other Side. Fighters against evil.

The words of Klea regarding Mother God on The Other Side:

She looks after everyone, like a mother should; she takes care of us. Azna is around all the time. She is very approachable. She has a good sense of humor, she is great.

ANGELS

Angels are everywhere, always around, singing is truly beautiful. Lots have wings, others do not.

I asked Klea how do you know they are angels?

Klea says:

Their look is different. They don't look like us. You just know.

AZNA'S VISIT

In my meditations I asked Mother God to cheer up Klea.

Klea:

Mother God came yesterday (our time) to visit. She said everything will be fine. Just don't worry. Azna smiled and waved her sword. I actually felt a lot better. She is so nice. She is great.

I asked Klea if Azna actually came to our home.

Klea was amazed:

That is correct baby. We are her children, she takes care of us.

So I said "Azna just waved her sword and you felt a lot better? I guess she considers us important."

Klea's response:

I don't know honey. It is you not me.

When Azna came to visit, Klea was shocked. That doesn't happen. It is all because of Ura.

MOTHER GOD'S APPEARANCE

I asked Klea what she looks like?

Klea's description:

Very beautiful, tall, skin like a tan but a milk white tone to it, long hair, buxom, blond hair, she shines, eyes like blue-green, big eyes, flowing gown, shimmers, white gown, blue shimmer too, almond shaped eyes, very striking eyes, you knew it was her, no one looks like her, ohh she is gorgeous, very beautiful, she stands out.

CHAPTER 16

FATHER GOD

The Godhead is Mother (Azna) and Father God. The Co-Creators of the universe. There has always been a Mother and Father God. Father is the intellect. He is pure maleness. Mother is the emotion. Father and Azna have constant overwhelming, unconditional love for all their creations, us their children. No matter how many mistakes we make in our incarnations and our Life Between Lives on The Other Side their ultimate love for us is constant, never changing. **Both Co-Creators are real physical entities.** The Holy Spirit is the love energy between Mother and Father God. Father God maintains stability and keeps everything in place in the universe.

On The Other Side as with Mother God, there is the Temple to Father God. It is a gigantic golden cathedral with golden doors, pink golden spires rising hundreds of feet in the air, and there is no cross on top. The stained glass windows have no holy pictures, no saints. The windows depict the trials and tribulations of humankind, such as: people gathering around a departed loved one, a mother holding a child, and words of wisdom by the messengers of God. Father's temple is not ornate with the exception of the golden pillars and the altar.

This altar has a golden mist around it. One feels they are alone with Father. One feels an overwhelming power of love on The Other Side by Father but especially here in his temple at the altar. Father's love is constant, encompassing and always channels knowledge. Giving Father God in history human traits by the organized religions of the world was totally irrational, it just created a false god because he is not human. The last few centuries Christianity focused on Jesus Christ and gave minimal attention to Father God.

Mother comes into physical form often and changes at will. She takes form easier and more frequently. Father maintains spirit form and can be everywhere. Rarely does he come into physical form. Father does not hold his form for long. He has too much power. He can take on any presence he chooses. Both have real physical form. Father in spirit form can be everywhere. It is foolish to think that he just resides in a church. Thus, if you want to pray or talk to Father one can do it anywhere.

In the rare situations on The Other Side when Father appeared in physical form this is how he has been described. He stands very tall with a stately stance with a blinding light that changes from silver to gold and then to purple. It has been said the light can actually hurt one's eyes. His coloring has been both dark and light with handsome beautiful features. As like Mother, a multicultural appearance, at times Hispanic, Asian, or Indian. Enormous eyes, beautiful hands and an angular figure. Father God has never appeared as an old man with a beard.

There are several locations on The Other Side in which a dome will come down over you, like a veil and you can have a private conversation with Father. When he speaks to you there is communication directly with the human mind. He mostly talks in a philosophical manner with the prime emphasis on love. He can counsel you but Mother is more direct and gives advice to you of a more personal nature. There have been numerous examples by prominent people that state it is a very strong male voice in your head but not in your head. What is said is very precise to the point with incredible intelligence that something you would never have thought of or ever think of saying. For this reason, one knows they would never think of saying this. It is definitely not coming from that person.

As Mother's army of angels are called Thrones, Father's angels are called Principalities. Both these phyla of angels have great powers. These angels are the highest, most elevated, and most spiritual. These angels are sent in times of danger and are especially protectors of children and animals. The Principalities have high intelligence, carry golden spears, and usually come in small groups of two or three. In contrast, Thrones come in larger groups. The Principalities are the sentinels, guardians of the world that emanate great protective power. Their power is immeasurable. Principalities can vanquish dark entities and any form of negativity. Their primary function is to be Father's army and to serve him.

The words of Klea about Father God:

Father God you feel his presence; you feel it, but you cannot see him, feel his presence, such a feeling of warmth and love; it is everywhere.

About 50 years ago our time; he did appear to everybody on The Other Side; they talk about it, say it was amazing, it rarely happens.

Father God doesn't get involved in your problems but Mother God does. There is such a great feeling of love with Father God.

I have not gone to the Temple of Father God, waiting till Ura returns HOME. Father God you feel but you do not see or hear him.

CHAPTER 17

THE PAST, THE VIOLENT HISTORY

Ideals are peaceful, history is violent. The history of humankind has been savage, cruel with extreme violence, at times with no mercy. It has been heart-wrenching with blood and the sacrifice of flesh with every human emotion expressed, of the thrill of victory, the agony of defeat, tears, sobbing, crying, the depths of despair, sorrow, and triumphs. The countless wars, battles on every continent of the world. The victorious marching armies of battles, the glory, amongst the defeated subjects, securing the spoils of victory with glory as always fleeting.

What if humankind actually knew in their conscious mind that no one ever actually died? All left their temporary basic physical body behind. This body is built for one life. Their consciousness, their total true self, instantaneously transferred to their eternal Astral or Etheric Body and all made the trip HOME. To fight another day in the future. Taking on a different temporary body here again. Across the ages the soul had many guises, faces but it was the same soul, still them. We are not our body here.

The effect on humankind if this information was known in the conscious mind in contrast to being stored in the subconscious mind would have been profound. So, why not divulge this information by Mother and Father God, our Co-Creators, in the evolution of our soul's spirituality?

When do we learn and remember our greatest lessons not when situations are ideal but in our darkest hour. There is a mandate for pain and suffering to learn our greatest lessons to advance the spirituality of the soul. We must feel the pain to understand protection. We must experience the tears to appreciate the laughter. We must learn the lessons of all the different manifestations of love, compassion, courage, forgiveness, gratitude, and to love one another. We must experience loss to appreciate gain. It is analogous to the sculpture of the sword into the fire by the blacksmith, at the end there is a magnificent sword, termed the soul. Our soul will be shaped by the fire closer to Mother and Father God. The true glory is at the end. What we do in life echoes in eternity.

No one, no soul ever died. The great wars through history from ancient times to the present, no one ever died. From the Civil War to the Great War of World War I, to the sequel war of World War II. December 7, 1941, a date which will live in infamy, the attack on Pearl Harbor, with 2,400 Americans killed that day. September 11, 2001, known as 9/11, 2,977 were killed. All traveled HOME to live another day. Taken HOME by Mother God's Angels, the Thrones.

All the different diseases, the infections, the plagues, the pandemics, cancer, heart disease, and so many other maladies that plagued humankind throughout the millennia across the world claimed countless lives. Or we thought it did. All these souls had their consciousness transferred to their Astral Bodies and traveled HOME to The Other Side. The higher energy dimension. The true reality dimension. A far superior replica of Earth compared to This Side.

All the souls of the universe ever created still exist

Knowledge that there is no death and the existence of The Other Side will be the greatest discovery in human history. In the next one hundred years research into human consciousness will open the doors to who and what we truly are. The realization that we are immortal interdimensional spirit beings as our Co-Creators Mother and Father God. This will have far reaching profound effects on This Side. Death is simply a change of address from this basic physical dimension on This Side to the Astral planes on The Other Side. Where we all came from, called HOME. We all go HOME in the end.

CHAPTER 18

THE DAILY LIFE OF KLEA AND URA

What is our daily life like now with Klea and I? Klea has returned HOME, on The Other Side but stays with me now 24/7. The only time she returns to The Other Side is when I take my afternoon nap, which she always kisses me on the head as I get settled in our recliner chair in the family room. The other time is when we retire to our bed upstairs when I go to sleep. Klea stays with me until I fall asleep then goes to The Other Side. However, during the night she continuously comes back and forth checking on me. Every night when I wake up, which is often, she is with me. I work many times in the late hours during the night or the wee hours of the morning, such as writing this book. She is always with me.

The transition back and forth between The Other Side and This Side is instantaneous; she just has to think it and it happens. This is travel across dimensions by thought power or projection.

Although our routine has changed often this is what a regular day is like for us now. In the morning when I wake up she is there in bed waiting for me. We go downstairs and sit in the recliner chair in the family room as I have my morning coffee. Klea and I first always do 'cuddle time,' which involves several forms of Target Clairsentience as described in our first book. For example, I ask her "Klea merge within me" I immediately receive a tremendous blast of waves of energy throughout my whole body. When one receives something as powerful as this it is impossible to forget or miss. If you never experienced this you will never know and understand. There is absolutely nothing like it in this life.

Then I will say "Klea total blending of our being," again a very strong blast of energy totally through me. The Clairsentience which we have been given by Mother and Father God is such a beautiful gift and blessing.

We also do now what we call a 'Total Toby.' When you go to the Reincarnation Chart one sees a life in 1806 A.D. Klea was my beautiful Toby and I was her handsome Kenneth. We were just married on route from Ireland to America and we perished at sea. When I say to Klea: "Let us do a Total Toby, Klea totally immerse within me." She puts on a light blue bonnet hat as per that time period. I have various images of her. She loves to say something about us. As an example, Klea says we had a wonderful Irish Wedding, we got on this ship sailing for America and drowned at sea. But, we went HOME together. Then I receive a very long, constant energy blast throughout my body. This is different from the other forms of Target Clairsentience because of the duration. The energy surge is steady and constant for at least 10 seconds.

We always follow up with an 'energy kiss.' I described this in our first book, in which I just receive waves of energy only on my face and mouth. Occasionally, we hold hands in which I just receive waves of energy in both hands up to my wrists.

THIS IS OUR GENERAL ROUTINE ON HOW WE START OUR DAY

Remember I can see her with my Clairvoyance and hear her with my Clairaudience, plus with the ever present powerful Clairsentience that was always our strongest gift. Every day I always do mind focus exercises to strengthen my psychic abilities and to open my Chakras as described in detail in our first book.

At this point we discuss our day and what we should do. Several hours per day we write our second book, in which I write things down verbatim, like a court recorder or stenographer. Our other daily activities involve cooking, shopping, and watching TV together. Klea is always with me now no matter what activity I am doing here on This Side. As I write this, she is standing looking over my shoulder.

There are countless examples of our conversations day or night. For instance, if we are shopping, Klea will instruct me to get this or you don't need that. Many times as I am cooking and would have made a mistake she tells me no, do not do that and gives me the reason why. She was the great cook. She would go into the kitchen and literally create magic, me as far as cooking, not so much. Thus, I always listen carefully to what she is telling me when I cook. Our conversations continue throughout the day and night.

Remember the transition HOME is simply the transfer of your consciousness, your total you, from your temporary body here to the eternal Astral Body. You still have your total personality, a higher mind because your conscious and subconscious minds have combined. Once you return HOME the amnesia blocks have been released. Klea still has that great sense of humor, many times we laugh so hard at the things we say to each other. We are like the 1950's TV show *George Burns and Gracie Allen.*

At night we go up to our bed together and have numerous conversations about all kinds of topics. Every night I always wake up and continue our conversations or go downstairs. There we will sit in the recliner chair in the family room and watch TV, or I may work in the dining room, or listen to late night music on a radio. My Klea in many respects is closer to me now than when she was with me here in this basic physical realm or This Side.

As described in our first book, we still do what I call our interdimensional pillow talk in our bed. Most of the discussions are about details on The

Other Side and our daily activities. Every night in bed we still 'spoon' where I turn on my right or left side and she cuddles up close to my back and every time I say "spoon honey," I receive a great Clairsentience blast just in my back. We do this several times. The intimacy is beyond description. We always do Target Clairsentience, merging in bed every night too with lots of conversational laughter.

Klea tells me her technique. She gets as close to me as possible then 'blasts' me. Klea has the image of her energy going into me. **Thought energy controls other forms of energy.** Let me tell you, this energy blast of Clairsentience, there is nothing in life like it. I wish I could transfer my consciousness so others will know and understand these incredible experiences, but this is something I cannot do. We live a very full active daily life of laughter, joy, and most of all, intense eternal love that inspired the title of our first book *For All Is Love.*

Soul Astral Travel

Let me introduce the concept known as Soul Astral Travel, which simply is your soul still attached to your temporary body here by the energy or silver cord then travels to The Other Side where you meet with loved ones, chat with your spirit guides, or just recharge your soul energy level.

I asked Klea about this Soul Astral Travel. She did not know if I did this during the night because she is often gone on The Other Side. However, in conversations with my Master Spirit Guide, I call Carl, he told me my Soul Astral Travel during the night occurs often because there have been many discussions on The Other Side as I sleep here.

CHAPTER 19

PRESENT REVELATIONS AND COMMUNICATION WITH THE OTHER SIDE

In my relentless research in all the medical, scientific, metaphysical, and spiritualism fields I discovered Azna, the Mother God. This greatly stimulated my interest but also I actually started to get angry. This was a new emotion in the last two years I never had in all my extensive research. I started my research on Mother God with books written by the world-renowned Medium and scholar of ancient religions, Sylvia Browne. Namely, her *Journey of the Soul Series: Books 1, 2 and 3* and her book devoted to Mother God.

WHY WAS SHE KEPT IN THE SHADOWS OF HISTORY?

In religious history it would have been unthinkable to have a woman deity of this omnipotent importance as a Mother God, a Co-Creator. This would have never, ever been allowed by the men throughout religious history to have a woman deity, a Mother God.

Remember the religions of the world in the past and present are still run and controlled by men. Tragically for thousands of years women were considered by men very low on the evolutionary scale. It would have been unthinkable to have a Mother God as the Co-Creator with Father God. So, why was I getting angry as I did more research on Azna? I thought at first it was just the injustice throughout history on This Side in keeping Mother God in the shadows, but I learned there was another reason that will be disclosed in the next chapter.

Now my communication with The Other Side has become quite extensive and varied. I have communication constantly with Klea, my five spirit guides, and the Council of Elder members. **Furthermore, I now have two-way conversations constantly with Mother God. Yes, you heard correctly.** I know this is really wild!!! However, I only can tell you the truth as humanly possible, analytical, and rational within my heart of hearts and soul. Much more will be revealed in the next chapter.

COMMUNICATION WITH MY SPIRIT GUIDES

First, let me introduce my Master Spirit Guide, I call Carl. Everyone has a Master Spirit Guide (MSG). Your MSG is always with you. At the time you take your first breath here on This Side to your last when you go HOME. He or she is your advisor, counselor, and best friend who knows everything about you in this life. The MSG functions only in an advisor role to keep you on track of your life chart objectives to advance your soul spirituality.

When you sleep at night the MSG will plant the seed of ideas and information into your subconscious mind to help you. Usually this information is projected into your right side, the receptive mind, the right hemisphere of the brain that surfaces up from the subconscious mind to the conscious mind. This is known as infusion. This is a major method how The Other Side infuses knowledge and ideas into our conscious mind.

Many other entities in addition to spirit guides can infuse information into your subconscious mind to ultimately surface into your conscious mind. Throughout recorded history the greatest achievements to benefit humankind have been derived by subconscious mind infusion from The Other Side. Thus, all those great ideas you thought came from you, guess what, most likely it came from your MSG and other entities.

As described in our first book, I have a team of five spirit guides: Carl my MSG, followed by Mike, Henry, Olivia, and Erica. Spirit guides come and go throughout your life depending on needs at times. Each spirit guide has a different area of responsibility. I currently have five spirit guides. It is quite unusual to have five. However, each one is here for specific needs at this juncture point in my present life here.

I have a regular meeting with my five spirit guides using a special form of meditation, visitation geared just for spirit guides. Every soul in this universe has their own specific energy vibration frequency. We communicate by Clairsentience, Clairaudience, and Clairvoyance. Our get-together occurs when I sit on the living room couch. I always see the five of them standing in front of me, in this order from my right to left: Carl, Mike, Henry, Olivia, and Erica. My Clairvoyance is very clear, I see when they laugh and smile at things I may say. I know exactly what each one looks like. It is like I am talking to any one of you in my living room.

By strong Clairaudience we communicate, have conversations, I ask questions, and I receive answers. Now we have advanced so far they ask me questions and I answer. Many times we actually laugh together. We have an excellent relationship. When I ask each one individually to step into my energy field, the Auric Field, the Clairsentience energy response is unique for each spirit guide. When I ask them to retreat from my energy field, I then feel my baseline energy or Auric Field. My spirit guides have told me my energy field is huge with great energy. When I ask all five to step into my energy field, the Clairsentience energy blast from all five is off the scale. It is simply tremendous. It is an additive effect. In addition, brief communications with my spirit guides at times also takes place at the end of my daily opening of the Chakras.

I now have a long history of seeing my Council of Elders by my Clairvoyance. As mentioned previously I have three: one woman and two men. These council members know me extremely well since I started with them at the incarnation process in the evolution of my soul long ago. At first I would see my council members in my meditations and visitations with angels, spirit guides, and of course my Klea always present. Furthermore, when I would do my daily psychic mind focus exercises and the opening of my Chakras, I would see my council members.

THE AGE OF AZNA

Through the ages Mother God has been kept in the shadows of history on This Side. For some unknown reason I was getting quite angry about this and strongly felt something should be done about the injustice to Mother God. I proposed in countless meditations and visitations to The Other Side that there should be a series of appearances by Azna throughout the world on This Side making the people or souls of This Side aware that there is a Mother God in addition to a Father God. We are all their children. Let all the souls on This Side know that they all have a Mother who has unconditional love for all of them. She fights and protects her children. She gives that special touch of love that only a mother can give.

I proposed a series of appearances by Azna for the people of the world on This Side with a strong message of who she is and to give them hope against all the evil and negativity on This Side. Additionally making absolutely sure that Mother God is not to be confused with the Blessed Mother in Christianity, the Mother of Jesus, as has happened in the past.

Thus, I declared to all on The Other Side, especially the Council of Elders, let us be the ones to usher in the Age of Azna. Let the souls on This Side know with great hope and love that they have a Mother God who is always there for them fighting against evil and negativity. That she is very active in helping them in their trials and tribulations here on This Side.

The end result was that I have weekly meetings with several members of the Council of Elders. Our purpose is planning and outlining a strategy for introducing Mother God to This Side. In these meetings with the council members I see them by my Clairvoyance and hear them by my Clairaudience. Thus, we can actually have conversations. There are many council members at these meetings and the woman of my personal council is the spokesperson. At present these meetings have been very productive in the development of a strategy to bring forth the Age of Azna to This Side.

The Age of Mother God.

CHAPTER 20

COMMUNICATION WITH MOTHER AND FATHER GOD

How Mother and Father God communicate with us is by a voice in our mind but not in our mind, in our head but not in our head. Bilocation of a soul is that one can be in two places at the same time. All souls can learn to do bilocation. Higher souls can be at multiple locations at once. For Mother and Father God there is an infinity of places they can be at the same time. Mother and Father are everywhere and can take on any form they choose.

My communication with Mother God is daily and continuous

I talk to her constantly mostly out loud but sometimes in my mind. She always answers directly right to the point with a strong touch of caring and love, like a mother should. Mother has a very distinctive female voice. It is strong and loving every time. I will ask her questions and she immediately answers. It is a very caring voice. It is certainly not my voice. One knows their own voice in your thoughts, in your head. It is certainly not me with a female voice in my head. Plus, she gives information I would never be aware of and uses phrases I simply would not use. One knows their own thoughts in their head.

Although the communication is daily with Mother God it would be best to focus on several of the most important and profound questions. Her answers astonished Klea and I, Ura, to an immeasurable degree to say the least. Klea can also hear Mother God when she speaks to me. Now my spirit guides can hear her voice when she talks to me too.

FIRST, LET ME ADD A DISCLAIMER HERE. People are never going to believe this!!! Plus, I am certainly not crazy and not hearing things and voices in my head. I am certainly not having auditory hallucinations. Well here we go! Answers from Mother God are verbatim.

TWENTY-FOUR QUESTIONS I ASKED MOTHER GOD

QUESTION #1: Mother, why was Klea and I, Ura, given these rare incredible gifts of communication: Clairsentience, Clairaudience, and Clairvoyance?

> Because son we wanted to make it easier for you by communicating with her. You are our son and we love you very much. Son is not symbolic of everyone it is actual, no you are truly our son!!! You are our son, both of us, Father too.

She told me I was her son many times. Now an explanation of what this means from Mother God. To our amazement which I have been told countless times, I, Ura, am the son of Mother and Father God. What do you say to something like that? Are you kidding me, yeah right? I am totally blown away, in total shock. After being told numerous times by Mother I still am in shock and totally amazed. Klea has the same feelings as I do. Plus, the word son used by Mother God is not symbolic of everyone but the real deal. Wow!! I still at times I cannot believe it. Do you know how difficult it is to believe something like this; me the medicine, science, Bronx guy? The no nonsense guy. However, after you have been told countless times and hit over the head many times, it starts to sink in.

This is not an illusion of grandeur because I know nothing of this. Remember everything is blocked off from my subconscious mind to my conscious mind by the amnesia blocks.

Thus, Klea and I were given these gifts because of who I am on The Other Side. At first I am thinking like in the movie the Matrix: You are the one!!! Laughing at first but I no longer laugh anymore. As I write this people are going to think ohh he is just crazy, and I would not blame them in the least. However, when you are constantly being told this by several sources on The Other Side including Mother herself, what do you say?

Putting all the pieces together why did I always have five Thrones around me? Normally people have a guardian angel but not five Thrones. Now I have eight around me. It just increased again to greater than eleven Thrones. I now have a small army of Thrones around me. My Master Spirit Guide, Carl, always wondered about this. Secondly, as I described in the last chapter of our first book, I had six instances of auto accidents and very serious illnesses in this life in which I walked away like nothing happened, not a scratch. These were totally outrageous, ridiculous, situations in which I should have certainly died. Now this is starting to become clear and putting everything together, I am very protected because I am the son of Mother and Father God.

When Klea first returned HOME, during the meeting with her Council of Elders, it was stated that Ura is very important and powerful. Furthermore, this highly powerful unique energy I possess that has been experienced by so many on The Other Side. Things start to add up.

My own personal opinion is no matter how much evidence is presented, this is too much of a credibility leap for people. Even for those who have worked in the Afterlife field for decades. Too many people are indoctrinated by the 'man-made' religious dogma.

Let's continue with Mother God's answers below.

QUESTION #2: Mother, are there other sons or daughters that you and Father have?

> No, we selected you when your soul was in an embryo or inception form. You are the only one.

Who would think of this as my soul in embryo or inception form???

QUESTION #3: Mother, why am I your only child?

> Because we designed tasks for you and it only required one. We did not need more than one.

QUESTION #4: Mother, how did you select me among the countless other souls in embryo form?

> We selected you because we knew your characteristics of being very loving, you were a warrior, very spiritual, and you would fight for justice.

QUESTION #5: Mother, when was my embryo form selected?

> Long ago before all creation of the universe was complete. We wanted someone with your characteristics.

This selection process took place before the creation of the universe was complete. Now this one really got me. **Before the universe was complete I was selected in my embryo form.**

I would never think of this!!! I would not know how to make this 'stuff' up. Who would think of something like this?

QUESTION #6: Mother, did you select Klea for me and if yes, why?

> Yes, son we selected Klea for you because she would give you stability through the ages. We knew you would have an eternal love with her. It was all about making you happy so there would be no problems with the tasks that had to be done.

Everything is a focus on the tasks that have to be done.

QUESTION #7: Mother, in my darkest hours of pain and suffering after Klea returned HOME why did you not come and comfort me?

> Son, I truly wanted to come but you were not ready. I was torn with emotion. I think it would have confused you.

QUESTION #8: Mother, numerous times in this life I was saved from certain death by illness and auto accidents. How was I saved from all this?

> You were protected by my Thrones. The Thrones would never let anything happen to you. They shield you from harm. The Thrones are always there for you. You are totally protected.

QUESTION #9: Mother, as I did relentless research on Mother God (Azna) why was I getting so angry at you being cast into the shadows of history on This Side, which has never happened before in all my extensive research?

Because you knew my son deep in your heart and soul that I was your mother.

Now there is something that requires clarification. In all our past lives we all have a mother in each life chosen by us in the creation of our life charts on The Other Side. However, Mother God is my eternal mother.

QUESTION #10: Mother, why was it kept secret for so long through the ages that I was your son?

> Because son we wanted you to be protected from the darkness, the evil out there. When you incarnate you are vulnerable, you can be hurt. We wanted to keep you safe. Now is the time you will be coming HOME to us for eternity.

I would never think of the concept that only when one is incarnate they are vulnerable to the darkness, the evil in the universe. Thus, when you are discarnate in spirit form you no longer are vulnerable to the darkness.

Let me add when there is someone important on The Other Side do you draw attention to them here on This Side or just keep it a secret to protect them?

QUESTION #11: I have been told numerous times by Klea and my Master Spirit Guide that Mother God will take me HOME herself. Later Mother God told me herself. This never happens when a person returns HOME that Mother God herself will take them HOME. Why me?

> Because you are my son and this is the last time you will take on life on Earth. It is appropriate that I take you HOME because this is your last time there.

QUESTION #12: Mother, when you come to take me HOME, you also said all will come and they will be shown. Is this correct?

All the angels will come, you will have your spirit guides with you, your Klea, then I will take your hand to take you HOME. It will be visible in your realm for all to see. It will be spectacular, my son. This will be the proof of who you really are. It will be such a joyous occasion.

Let me add when Mother comes herself to take me HOME so This Side will see, that will be the proof that I am truly her son.

QUESTION #13: Mother, why was I given this incredible powerful energy that flows through me?

It was given to you by myself and Father God, as a gift of our love for you. This energy will be important for the tasks ahead. It will be important for what has to be done. It is all about the tasks that have to be done.

So Mother and Father God are going to put me to work. Well, I guess no retirement for me when I return HOME on The Other Side. Again, it is all about the tasks that await me.

QUESTION #14: Mother, do the tasks ahead involve the darkness in the universe?

Yes son, absolutely. There is a plan we devised long ago designed for you.

QUESTION #15: Mother, recently the darkness tried to reach me and the Thrones protected me. Why did the darkness try to reach me and is the darkness afraid of me?

> Here incarnated you are vulnerable my son. But once you return HOME as discarnate you are no longer vulnerable to the darkness and the darkness is afraid of your energy.

Now this incredible powerful energy I possess has been described in a previous chapter by so many on The Other Side: Klea, spirit guides, council members, and enjoyed very much by the Presence and the angels. And what is the purpose of the gift given me by Mother and Father God of this exceptional energy? It is for the tasks waiting for me.

QUESTION #16: Mother, I have been thinking about how we become young again as we enter the tunnel that takes us HOME to The Other Side. Does the tunnel have an energy that restores our youth or is it all from the transfer of consciousness to the Astral Body?

> No son, the tunnel is an energy field that restores cellular vitality. The Astral Body is part of it but it is primarily the tunnel effect. It is more complicated than this but this answer should suffice. The tunnel is much more than a transfer point from This Side to The Other Side.

In the vast literature about the tunnel it is always viewed as the bridge between realms of This Side to The Other Side. The tunnel is never discussed about being an energy field to reverse the aging process as one returns HOME.

QUESTION #17: Mother, how were the souls in the universe created?

The souls were created all at the same time. We then allowed conditions for the souls to develop their own characteristics. The souls were created in pods with two souls to a pod, one female, the other male. There is much more but this will suffice as an answer.

The only thing I have to say to this answer, who would ever think of this?

QUESTION #18: Mother, how were all the souls in the universe created at the same time?

> The souls were created from the uncreated matter of the universe. There is an enormous cloud of uncreated matter in the universe. This uncreated matter was separated from the remainder and was divided up to create the pods the souls were in.

QUESTION #19: Mother, about these pods. There is a female and male soul in these pods, are these your twin souls?

> Yes son, each pod has a male and female presence which is your twin soul. Twin flame has also been used. It is the representation of the universe of a male and female presence. The twin soul is you occupying the same pod.

So twin souls are 'pod partners' composed of a female and male from inception.

QUESTION #20: Mother, tell me about these pods?

> These pods are like small incubators. It is a 'hatching process.' Everything that the soul needs to develop is supplied. We have no

time here, it is not time dependent. The pods are made of a spiritual substance of energy. It is a total life giving energy. It is similar to ectoplasm but not ectoplasm.

Ectoplasm is a supernatural viscous substance that is supposed to exude from the body of a Medium in trance and form the material for the manifestation of spirits.

QUESTION #21: Mother, this powerful energy I have, will this energy flow through a sword?

Yes son, this powerful energy will be transmitted through a sword against the darkness.

I am speechless. How would I even know to ask these questions?

It will be the sword of justice against the darkness of the universe. Justice will come to the universe.

QUESTION #22: Mother, this extremely powerful energy that flows through me from you and Father that has affected so many on The Other Side what is the nature of this energy? I feel this energy getting stronger within me. No one on The Other Side ever experienced this energy before.

Son, this energy comes from the Celestial Realm not from the lower Astral spheres. It is an extremely high vibrating energy form, from Father and I that will pierce through everything. The darkness will be vanquished with this energy. The angels and the Presence know what this energy is because they are from the Celestial Realm. This energy will get progressively stronger within you because you are getting closer to the tasks at hand.

Clarification is needed here. The universe is composed of countless spheres, dimensions, and realms. The highest is the Celestial Realm. Most souls are in the lower realms in the Astral planes.

I will be ready Mother.

I know you will son.

QUESTION #23: Mother, how was the universe created?

An enormous cloud of matter was created. I and Father used a series of different forms of energy on parts of this uncreated matter. Different forms of energy were used to create suns and planets. Energy sculptured the matter. Energy transforms matter. There is an infinity of forms of energy having different effects on matter. The universe was created sector by sector. To create the conditions for life the matter, which made up the suns and planets, was acted upon by various forces and energy. This is a very general description.

QUESTION #24: Mother, tell me about consciousness in the Universe and how many dimensions or realms are in the Universe?

Father and I wanted to have instant communication and connection throughout the Universe so we created consciousness that would be everywhere and permeate in the Universe.

Son, there are countless dimensions in the Universe. Each dimension has their own form of consciousness. Within each dimension there are 'subforms' of consciousness. The degree of consciousness is unlimited in the Universe because spirit beings create their own consciousness. **Consciousness is the communication system of the universe.**

There you have it. I know this is very wild and tests the outer limits of what people believe. Their belief systems will get challenged to a very high degree. I know this sounds like something out of a science fiction movie. What is this something out of the movie Star Wars?

The obvious question is how would I even know any of this information? The short answer is no way!!!

Mother and I communicate continuously and she tells me she is always there for me, which she is. We are always talking like a mother to a son, and a son to a mother. Mother and I have such strong bonds. Mother communicates with me on several levels, the conscious mind, the subconscious mind, images, telepathic pathways of thoughts. It is an astounding bond of communication. Thoughts? Trust me as I am writing this, I am saying to myself people are never going to believe this, never!!! People are going to take the easy way out and just say well this guy is just 'nuts.' However, the proof will be the teaching moment of my return HOME with Mother taking me HOME.

She has a great sense of humor and we make each other laugh all the time. Remember laughter is nourishment for the soul. People always have the impression when you talk about the Afterlife everything always has to be so serious. That is simply not the case on The Other Side. Humor is the great gift to rise above what can be seen as tragedy. Sometimes Mother and I get emotional. We have this eternal, unbreakable bond that is an incredible blessing.

I know whatever the tasks that lie ahead, I, Ura, as son of Mother and Father God will give all my very being of my heart and soul to be victorious to the end. It is unthinkable to ever disappoint Mother and Father. I hope I will always be worthy of their faith and trust in me.

COMMUNICATION WITH FATHER GOD

There have been countless references in history when Father God speaks to you. It is a very strong, powerful male voice in your head but not in your head. A voice of sheer maleness. An acute omnipotent intelligence of few words but to the point as with Mother's communications. You can feel the love of Father as with Mother, communication with both is a humbling and exhilarating experience beyond any description.

Since I just shocked you about my communications with Mother God, here comes the second shock: my communications with Father God.

It was November 5, 2020 at 1:35 am. As I write this I just realized it was the second year anniversary of my beautiful Klea going HOME. When Father God was communicating with me, this fact was lost to me, maybe because I was so stunned by the event. However, as I write this now I am shocked by this powerful synchronicity.

The setting of this direct communication with Father God is: I am working into the night as I often do on my computer in the dining room. For some unexplained reason I say out loud "how am I doing?" To this day I have no idea why I said this out loud.

The following: a very powerful voice spoke to me in my head but not in my head and said:

> **You are doing fine my son. You were chosen long ago to be one of my soldiers. No one, nothing can harm you. I have tasks for you.**

The voice came from outside my head but then in my head. My first reaction was I was totally stunned. I never would talk like that. I know my voice in my head. This was not my voice. This never happened before, ever. This voice certainly did not come from me. At the time I was on the computer thinking of other things. The contents of this message was the furthest thing from my mind. I would have never thought to say "You were chosen long ago to be one of my soldiers." I never would phrase a message like that. I don't think or talk like that. In a few sentences everything was answered.

It was a very strong, male voice, a very powerful message with great intelligence. I know the tenor of my voice in my head and how I phrase things. This certainly was not my inner voice. This was not me. Father God sought me out to directly send me this message.

As previously mentioned on The Other Side there are several locations of domes of communication with Father God where one can go. This was not on The Other Side in a dome of communication with Father God. It was right here on This Side in my dining room of our home. After a while still stunned and in shock, I lay in bed thinking and thinking about this direct communication with Father God.

Repeating and repeating over in my mind "You were chosen long ago to be one of my soldiers. I have tasks for you."

CHAPTER 21

THE RETURN OF URA

Life here on This Side is very brief, temporary like our basic inferior bodies of lesser matter, built for one life. Life here is always fleeting. We all return HOME, whence where we originally came from. I, Ura, son of Mother and Father God will return HOME soon. Here now in this life is my final incarnation. Held secret by Mother and Father God through the ages my true identity for my protection against the darkness of the universe. Protecting me from harm in the times of my 62 incarnations.

Mother God, my mother will personally take her son HOME. I have been told countless times from The Other Side by Klea, my Master Spirit Guide, and now by Mother God herself. That Mother will take me HOME and there will be a spectacular demonstration at the moment of returning HOME to show those loved ones of the true reality. The true power, the unconditional love of Mother God. **That there truly is a Mother God.**

It has been said to me "all will come" on the return of Ura. The spirit guides will surround me, my Klea will stand by my side, Virtue Angels will line the path of the tunnel, Thrones will be there, Dominion Angels will greet me as I exit the tunnel to enter The Other Side. There will be many angels in honor of my spirituality. Mother God will come on This Side and take my hand and take me HOME for eternity. I have been told countless times there will be a great celebration of unlimited joy, happiness, and love by countless people on The Other Side.

This will be my final trip HOME, never to return, never to incarnate on This Side, we call Earth ever again. I, Ura, my soul since inception, was the warrior and teacher in the service of Mother and Father God for the greater good of the universe. I, Ura, will always protect what matters most in the universe with the guidance, power, and wisdom of Mother and Father God.

We are the light. We will always vanquish the darkness in the universe. I, Ura, was chosen long ago to be one of the soldiers of Mother and Father God. I know whatever tasks are ahead for me when I return HOME that we will be the ones standing in the end over the darkness. I swear it, with every part of my being in my heart and soul for all eternity.

As more revelations are being revealed I am starting to feel now that for the last two years of this spiritual journey that there is a master plan in the universe unfolding that is much bigger than Klea and I, Ura, realize. More than we can comprehend. Sometimes I question my own intelligence.

Mother's responses to my questions verbatim:

Ura: Why didn't I see this?

> You are very intelligent but everything is blocked off. How would you know? The future is the past. Everything occurs at once my son. Everything was planned and designed for you. There is so much more. You will see.

Ura: Mother will I see before I return HOME to you and Father?

Some you will learn but much more after you return HOME to us son. Father will communicate with you in the future between now and when you come HOME.

Ura: I put everything in your hands, Mother and Father.

You are our son, we will always do what is best for you. We love you very much.

I, Ura, place all my heart and soul into the hands of Mother and Father God. As this master plan is unfolding I go forth with courage, honor, and one in love with Mother and Father. I learned my ancient name means 'loved from the heart.' Thus, Father will contact me again before I return HOME.

The return of Ura to The Other Side, the dimension of the true reality, our HOME. When I Cross The Veil, where the many angels will welcome me back, surrounded by my five spirit guides, and my twin soul, Klea. Mother God will take her son's hand to lead him HOME for all eternity. It is my destiny. It has been such a long wait through the ages, even before the completion of the universe. It is not the end but a new beginning for all eternity. A new dawn will rise in the universe.

CHAPTER 22

LETTER TO MOTHER AND FATHER GOD

Thank you for entrusting in me the strength, the conviction for the tasks in this journey now and when I return HOME to you.

Thank you that I am worthy of your faith in me and it would be unthinkable to disappoint you. I will give my heart and soul to be worthy of your faith in me for the tasks ahead.

Thank you for guiding me straight, true, never wavering against the obstacles in my path. For keeping me resolute when all around me seemed lost.

Thank you for your protection and the signs along the way of this journey. Knowing for the good I have done. To be strong, to have honor for the tasks that await me.

Knowing I have done just and righteous with my time here on Earth through the many past lives down through the ages.

To return HOME for the last time with my head held high. I will always be resolute in the fight over the darkness, for we are the light.

Knowing in the end we will be the ones standing against the darkness in the universe. It will be the sword of justice against the darkness. A new dawn will rise in the universe.

I will always keep the faith for all eternity.

There will never be enough love for you.

I, your chosen soldier long ago before the completion of the universe.

Your son,
Ura

Appendix – The Reincarnation Chart

PRESENT	Felecia and Leonard – **New York, USA** – two sons
1903 AD	**Italy,** Angelina and Emilio – lived in the village of Sant'Angelo di Piove di Sacco – two children – one son and one daughter
1806 AD	**Ship at sea** (Atlantic Ocean) - Toby and Kenneth, on route from Ireland to America....Just married, we were so young, no children.....Perished at sea
1736 AD	**England** – Clare and Benjamin – had one child…a daughter
1642 AD	**Germany** – Safha and Tandel – had three children – three daughters
1541 AD	**Spain** – (The Renaissance) – Ana and Franco – had two children – one son and one daughter
703 AD	**Lithuania** (before it was Lithuania) Myrath and Raj – had five children – one still born – three daughters and one son
535 AD	**Honduras** (before it was called Honduras, in Central America) – Rotta and Tiko – had five children – four sons and one daughter
135 AD	**Mesopotamia** – Atta and Vebra – had three sons – Mesopotamia was an ancient region in the Eastern Mediterranean Sea, bordered by the Zagros Mountains in the northeast, composed of mostly present day Iraq, but also Turkey, Iran, and Syria
207 BC	**Rome, Italy** - Antonia and Claudius – two children – one son and one daughter
1038 BC	**Crimean Peninsula** in the Black Sea (Ukraine, before the name Crimea) – Tika and Noak had six children – three sons and three daughters
3016 BC	**Ancient Egypt** – Mira and Ptolemy – had four children – three sons and one daughter
5050 BC	**Samara Civilization** **(5th Millennium BC, Upper Volga River, Russia)** – Ena and Farouk – six children – four daughters and two sons

Three Past Lives In The Stone Age

7543 BC	Neolithic Period or New Stone Age
10009 BC	Cusp of the Paleolithic, Old Stone Age and Mesolithic, Middle Stone Age
15043 BC	The Old Stone Age, our first life together here

🍎 NOTES

❦ NOTES

❦ NOTES

❦ NOTES

❦ NOTES

❦ NOTES

❦ NOTES

❦ NOTES

❦ NOTES

❧ NOTES

Made in the USA
Las Vegas, NV
24 July 2021